6⁵²

Dance
Training for
Gymnastics

Rae Pica
Moving & Learning
Rochester, New Hampshire

Leisure Press
Champaign, Illinois

Library of Congress Cataloging-in-Publication Data

Pica, Rae, 1953–
   Dance training for gymnastics / Rae Pica.
     p.   cm.
   Bibliography: p.
   Discography: p.
   Includes index.
   ISBN 0-88011-306-5
   1. Gymnastics.   2. Dancing—Study and teaching.   I. Title.
GV461.P616 1988   87-31862
796.4'1—dc19   CIP

Developmental Editor: Judy Patterson Wright, PhD
Production Director: Ernie Noa
Projects Manager: Lezli Harris
Copy Editor: Claire Mount
Assistant Editor: JoAnne Hutchcraft Cline
Proofreader: Laurie McGee
Keyboarder: Kathy Fuoss
Typesetter: Theresa Bear
Text Design: Keith Blomberg
Text Layout: Denise Mueller
Cover Design: Conundrum Designs
Illustrations By: Dawn Bates
Interior Photos: Dave Black, Jack Adams
Printed By: Braun-Brumfield

ISBN: 0-88011-306-5

Printed in the United States of America

10 9 8 7 6 5 4 3 2 1

Leisure Press
A Division of Human Kinetics Publishers, Inc.
Box 5076, Champaign, IL 61820
1-800-342-5457
1-800-334-3665 (in Illinois)

This book is dedicated to the memory of my father, Raymond Joseph Pica, who, by his example, taught me that with enough determination anything is possible.

Acknowledgments

I'd like to offer sincere thanks to

my illustrator, Dawn Bates, who is a delight to work with;

publisher Rainer Martens of Human Kinetics, for suggesting I write this book;

my developmental editor, Judy Patterson Wright, for her intelligent and thoughtful comments and recommendations, her sense of humor, and her time and dedication;

Denise Gula, for her suggestions;

International Gymnast Magazine, which provided a forum for my first thoughts on the topic of dance for gymnastics;

New England Sports Academy in Madbury, New Hampshire, where I was first introduced to gymnastics;

Coach Gail Goodspeed and the Wildcat women's gymnastics team at the University of New Hampshire;

Sheila Chapman, for having provided a sympathetic ear and loving encouragement since we were in the eighth grade;

my family, for being my "fan club";

and my husband, Richard Gardzina, for being the kind of husband he is.

Contents

Preface

The controversy continues: Is artistic gymnastics sport or art form? Is the floor routine an exhibition in tumbling skills, or is it more like a choreographed dance in which tumbling also plays a part? Must gymnasts who love to tumble and vault and kip really have dance training? The intention of this book is to answer all of these questions and to show, without doubt, that dance is indeed a part of gymnastics. Gymnastics, although to the dismay of some, is most certainly *both* sport and art.

The idea for this book came about after several years of teaching dance to gymnasts and two years of writing about the subject for *International Gymnast Magazine*. The teaching happened almost accidentally, when I stopped at a gym to inquire about using the facility to conduct classes for children and adults. The director indicated it might be time for members of the competitive teams to begin having some dance training, and I was intrigued by the thought of combining dance and gymnastics. I'd watched gymnastics on television and found it terribly exciting, and I could always tell which of the competing gymnasts had had dance training.

So I was later appalled to discover the lack of written information on the topic of dance for gymnastics. How was I to know exactly what sort of training I should give the gymnasts? What should I include in my lesson plans? And, given that television commentators constantly refer to gymnasts' talents—or lack thereof—in dance, why wasn't there more information available on the subject?

But an even greater shock was learning that my students weren't interested in what I had to teach them. I then realized that if I wanted to teach dance to gymnasts, I'd have to either do it against their will or find a way to make it enjoyable for them.

This book is written for gymnasts, coaches, and dance instructors and is intended to define clearly the role of dance—ballet, jazz, modern, and even movement education—in gymnastics. For those who remain unconvinced that dance training should be part of the sport of gymnastics, this book will offer convincing arguments. For those already aware of the need for dance training, this book supplies information with regard to specifics—what kind of dance training, how much, and how it can be provided. It shows how the above-mentioned dance forms should be—and already are—used in gymnastics. The book discusses the role of dance in the choreography of floor and beam routines, and addresses the issue of dance for male gymnasts who have only just begun to be part of the controversy.

I have designed this book to be read by gymnasts at all skill levels, in the hope that they will come to understand fully the critical role of dance in gymnastics and to accept the need for training in dance technique. It is written for coaches at all levels who would like a greater awareness of the dance training they require of their gymnasts. The following chapters should prove to be a valuable aid in choosing dance instructors and in outlining the lesson contents for those instructors. They are intended for dance teachers interested in or presently working with gymnastics, and especially for those without a gymnastics background who would otherwise have to search for information through numerous texts and still have to proceed on a trial-and-error basis, as I did. Finally, this book will also prove helpful to the parents of gymnasts seriously interested in improving their craft. Should the necessary dance training not be available at their child's gym, parents who've read this book will have a greater knowledge of what they should seek in dance training for their young gymnasts.

Chapter 1

To Dance or Not to Dance?

© Dave Black

It has been estimated that, in women's gymnastics, dance comprises approximately 50 percent of floor exercise and balance beam routines. Not including the positive effects that dance technique can have on performances in vaulting and uneven bars, this would mean that dance makes up 25 percent—or one-quarter—of women's gymnastics.

This estimate is based on a number of factors. Among them is the reality that dance steps have long been regarded as the most useful tools in making the transitions between tumbling passes and other gymnastic elements. (The larger the gymnast's dance repertoire, therefore, the larger the selection of interesting movements and the more exciting the performance.)

Furthermore, there are numerous movements designated as "gymnastic difficulties" by the International Federation of Gymnastics (FIG) *Code of Points* that belonged to the world of dance long before they were considered gymnastic elements. Included in this category are many steps (leaps, turns, and jumps, to cite a few) also found in compulsory routines established by the United States Gymnastics Federation (USGF). In fact, the latest Class III compulsory floor routine, for example, contains 16 dance steps!

Finally, the floor and balance beam exercises are often said to be actually little more than choreographed dances, in which tumbling and other gymnastic skills also play a role. This description is justified by the fact that, in these two events, the gymnast performs not one skill, but a series of skills strung together in such a way as to create both fluency and continuity. The routines, in other words, must flow as a dance flows.

It is no surprise, therefore, that most coaches now agree that formal dance instruction should play a significant role in gymnastics training. Yet the gymnasts themselves don't always concur, most likely because they view dance as something separate from their sport and, for the most part, a waste of valuable time and effort that could be better spent learning new tricks. These sentiments are slowly changing, as the sport of gymnastics is itself changing. The trend is now toward a mixture of gymnastic skills and dance finesse.

Of course, when contemplated from the gymnasts' perspective, the argument does have a certain logic. After all, they have chosen gymnastics as an extracurricular activity. If they'd been interested in ballet, jazz, and modern dance, they would be spending their afternoons in a dance studio and not at a gym.

They can further argue that they're already learning and performing those dance skills that are required parts of their compulsory routines. These skills are covered, out of necessity, during training and practice sessions. Why, then, must additional time be spent on them during a dance class? Why must precious time be spent learning *basic* dance skills when they're already performing *advanced* dance skills on floor and beam?

Gymnasts are expected, very early in their careers, to perform steps that in a dance studio are commonly considered advanced skills. But coaches, as well as gymnasts, must ask themselves how well those advanced skills are being performed. Are feet always pointed when they should be? Are landings finished in *plié* (pronounced PLEE-AY)? Are knees tight and legs straight when they're supposed to be? Do the movements flow? Are the gymnast's personality and abilities fully expressed?

Quality training in dance technique will help ensure that the answer to all of these questions is an emphatic *yes*. However, because pointed toes and tight knees may not be reason enough to convince gymnasts (and those coaches who are still undecided), this chapter will highlight some additional benefits derived from dance training.

Hands and Arms

Among the list of questions that coaches should ask is, How well is the gymnast using all body parts, especially hands and arms? Though this may seem trivial in relation to the overall performance of strenuous and intricate skills, it must be remembered that each part contributes to the whole. Being conscious of these subtleties gives a marvelous display of talent a polished look. Without them, the performance sometimes seems unfinished. Usually, this somewhat unfinished appearance can be directly attributed to flaws involving hands and arms (Pica, 1984b). Failure to pay attention to these body parts results in

- arms hanging at the sides of the body like forgotten appendages;
- arms that "break" at the wrists, leaving hands to dangle, destroying what should be an unbroken line from shoulder to wrist;
- hands grasping at the air;
- fingers stretched and spread to their limit;
- arms pulled to the back, pinching shoulder blades together;
- shoulders hunched to the ears; and
- hands held in a balletic position regardless of the style of movement being performed.

Beyond appearance, and of even greater consequence, is the effect that arms and hands can have on performance itself. Arms that dangle or are thrown back beyond the body's midline will result in a loss of the natural balance that is of the utmost importance to a gymnast in every event and every movement. Inattention to the arms will also prevent the gymnast from attaining the greatest possible height in leaps and jumps.

Dance training requires students to concentrate on both body lines and body parts. A good deal of the training is spent on hands and arms. First and foremost, ballet training calls the gymnast's attention to the trapezius muscle in the back. This large, flat, triangular muscle on both sides of the back is responsible for controlling the arms. By expanding the back (as one does when taking a deep breath) and using it to lift and lengthen these limbs, the gymnast achieves the desired line to the arms, beginning at the spine and flowing through the shoulders to the fingertips. Although uncomplicated, it is generally only through regular ballet training that such usage becomes habitual. (Because it prevents the arms from tiring too quickly, students expected to extend one or both arms for long minutes at a time are usually grateful to discover the trapezius!)

Dance instruction also obligates students to perform with shoulders lowered and relaxed. Because arms are an important factor in almost all choreography, dance students soon learn to give equal consideration to these limbs in everything they do. They learn, too, that there is a hand position to accompany a jazzy style of movement. Unlike the rounded, closed, balletic hand, a jazz hand consists of a flattened palm, with fingers apart and energy almost visibly flowing from the fingertips.

Moreover, the use of a new or different arm or hand position can add an exciting element to the most common of movements and skills. Dance instructors, therefore, should allow for ample experimentation with both the elements of movement and the various movement qualities (refer to chapters 4 and 5), using arms and hands alone. Through such experimentation, gymnasts will discover that their upper limbs can move slowly or quickly, lightly or with great force, in a smooth and flowing or a sharp and punctuated manner, and in a variety of directions. They can also take on any number of shapes.

Similarly, combining pantomime (that first cousin to dance) with certain nonlocomotor skills is also extremely helpful in broadening one's use of hands and arms. Hands and arms can take on many characteristics; one can pretend to push and pull various objects; lift both heavy and light, small and large, and hot and cold materials; or strike in different ways (as though beating against a stuck door, hammering a nail, or swatting a fly). That, in turn, results in a greater awareness of these body parts and spawns ideas for their use during optional routines.

For the youngest gymnasts (preschool and preteam), instructors can guarantee a good start by having them perform hand and finger activities. These might include "Where Is Thumbkin?", or a game in which fingers emerge from and return to a closed fist, one at a time and at differing tempos. There are also many poems and songs dedicated to the multifaceted uses of hands and fingers. Young gymnasts who have spent considerable time miming the hands' numerous "jobs" (e.g., praying, beckoning, patting, scolding, playing piano, directing traffic, saying goodbye, etc.) are not likely to grow up taking these body parts for granted, nor are they likely to forget their existence during performances!

Faces and Heads

Although not as dramatically noticeable as hands and arms, use of the face and head is another technique that competing gymnasts can draw from dance training. It's true that gymnasts in the midst of a competition are bound to be preoccupied with, if not nervous about, their performance. Under these conditions, it's hard to smile during a routine. What gymnasts can learn from dance is that facial expression and head movement not only enhance but are actually essential to a well-executed and well-received performance. It's no wonder, then, that excitement mounts when these two qualities are witnessed from the bleachers and judges' seats!

If gymnasts thoroughly explore the six movement qualities (chapter 5)—this time with the head alone—they will feel considerably more comfortable with this body part. They will discover that a head can swing, and it can move in a slow, sustained manner. It can suspend, or it can collapse to the chest, shoulder, or back. It can be used percussively, with short, sharp movements, and it can vibrate or shake. These movements not only add to the expression of a piece, but also contribute to rhythmic variety.

With ballet training, gymnasts soon discover that the head and even the eyes play a vital role in creating that all-important visual body line. The line that a dancer or gymnast presents while performing steps or posing can make a vast difference in whether or not the audience's response is favorable. According to Gail Grant's (1982) *Technical Manual and Dictionary of Classical Ballet*, "A dancer is said to have a good or bad sense of line according to the arrangement of head, body, legs and arms in a pose or movement.

A good line is absolutely indispensable to the classical dancer'' (p. 70). The same can be said for the gymnast.

Training in jazz dance can also be especially helpful where the head is concerned. Whereas ballet tends to concentrate on body lines, jazz emphasizes the isolation and use of individual body parts. The head is one body part that has a major function in jazz dance (refer to "Head Isolations" in chapter 3).

With regard to use of the face, mime can once again be quite beneficial. Gymnasts should experiment with the many emotions faces can display, as a whole or through the use of its individual parts. When they are choreographing routines, gymnasts should consider the possibilities for the lift of an eyebrow, a sudden smile, or the lowering of eyes. Though such movement may be difficult for the more inhibited young gymnast to master and is likely to be forgotten with the excitement and tension of early competitions, repeated reminders from coaches can go a long way toward making the dance instructor's job easier. And just as constant reminders to *plié* or to point toes eventually pay off, so, too, will reminders to smile and use facial expressions.

It should also be noted that, as with hands and arms, there is more at stake with the proper use of the head and face than expression alone. This is because the eyes and head play such a vital role in turning, which is a major part of every gymnast's floor and beam routines. Although *spotting* is a term known to gymnasts as the method by which their coaches provide physical assistance, the word has an altogether different meaning in the dance studio. To *spot* while turning is to focus the eyes on a fixed point, at eye level and in line with the desired path. As a turn begins, and for as long as is physically possible, the eyes remain on the point chosen. As soon as the point disappears from view, the head whips around in order to find it again. The head, therefore, begins the turn later than does the rest of the body, but is the first body part to complete it.

Spotting should be practiced regularly as part of all forms of dance training. Its benefits to both dancers and gymnasts are threefold: (a) it helps prevent dizziness during turning, (b) it aids in maintaining balance, and (c) it keeps the performer on a straight and steady course toward the ultimate destination.

Injury Prevention

Perhaps the single greatest argument that can be made for quality dance training is the role it can play in injury prevention (Pica, 1984a). Though dance and safety in gymnastics may seem to have little in common, the fact is that instruction in dance technique will help bring about the proper execution of gymnastic skills. This proper execution can only result in fewer injuries. In addition, dance training prevents injury by strengthening and conditioning muscles that gymnastics training may ignore.

Good posture, or correct body alignment, is where it all begins (see Figure 1.1). Without it, bodies will either sag or arch; and when bodies aren't controlled, movements can't be either. Not only are

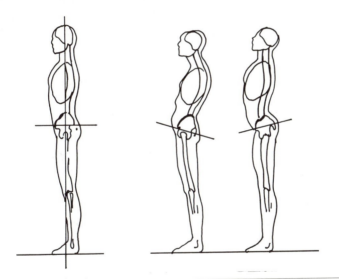

Figure 1.1   Correct and incorrect body alignment

uncontrolled bodies potentially hazardous, but when body parts are not properly aligned, unnecessary strain is also placed on muscles and joints. Poor alignment, in fact, is one of the major causes of muscle pulls and strains (Jacob, 1981). Proper execution of three dance basics—*plié, relevé,* and turn-out—can help prevent injuries and improve overall body alignment.

Understanding Plié

The dance student immediately begins to gain a sense of correct body alignment with the *plié*, which means "to bend" the knees, and is a basic skill practiced during the warm-up in all three dance techniques. Whether performed in turn-out (the outward rotation of legs and feet) or with the legs and feet parallel, when the knees bend, they must press out over the toes. The hips remain in line with the heels, and the body's weight is distributed evenly over all five toes and the back of the heels.

The two most common errors in the performance of this movement that must be corrected instantly are the buttocks protruding to the back and a rolling in of the feet. The former, of course, necessarily causes the back to arch and can eventually result in lordosis, or swayback, which is seen much too frequently in gymnasts and dancers who haven't learned to keep their buttocks tucked under. Besides being unattractive from an aesthetic point of view, swayback can also affect proper breathing and cause a muscular imbalance that further aggravates the problem (Gelabert, 1964).

When the feet roll in toward one another (with the small toes lifting off the floor), there is a great deal of strain being placed on the arches and the inner parts of the knees. *Pliés* (and other movements) performed this way can eventually lead to knock-knees and a lowering of the inner arch of the foot, both of which are very difficult to correct (Arnheim, 1980). Also, from a technical standpoint, the gymnast should realize that the elevation of leaps and jumps will suffer both when the entire foot is not used to push off the floor or beam and when the leap or jump is not originated with a *plié*.

The *plié*, of course, is also necessary upon landing from a leap, jump, vault, or dismount. In every landing, the force of gravity is at work, bringing the full weight of the body down to meet the landing surface. Therefore, if the knees don't bend when the feet hit an unyielding surface, the legs feel the impact. This can cause a jarring of the bones and cartilage in the knee, resulting in contusions or tears. In hyperextended knees, it can cause torn ligaments. In rare cases, improper landings can even cause knee ligaments to rupture (Jacob, 1981).

A straight-legged landing can also result in ankle injury and/or strain to the hamstring muscles. In some instances, the force can travel up the legs, through the pelvic girdle, and into the spinal column, causing injury to the lower back. Here, again, good posture is critical. When body parts are aligned, the stress of a landing is absorbed equally throughout the body, from feet to head.

Both instructors and students need to pay special attention to the *plié* until it becomes as comfortable and natural as breathing.

Understanding Relevé

The *relevé* (a rise onto the ball of the foot) is also regularly practiced in dance classes. It's an excellent exercise in balance, with balance and safety certainly being synonymous, and it provides gymnasts with a better feel for the use of the whole foot. Rather than moving entirely flat-footed or on tiptoe, gymnasts with the ability to make use of the whole foot are able to isolate toe from ball from heel. Such isolation enables them to grip the floor or beam for strength and balance when necessary and to leave those surfaces with greater spring.

In addition, gymnasts who've mastered the use of the whole foot are far less likely to perform flat-footed landings, which can also result in injury to the calves and shins. According to Raoul Gelabert (1964), "The less weight the feet are required to bear, the more they will be spared the stresses and strains of the...use to which they are put. . . . The better the body balance, the more easily the weight will fall correctly on the strongest part of the feet" (p. 51).

Understanding Turn-Out

Turn-out is yet another term heard often by both gymnasts and dancers. Although gymnasts are frequently instructed to perform various movements in turn-out, they're seldom given the opportunity to acquire turn-out gradually or to understand the mechanics involved. If they turn out the feet and lower legs, leaving the rest of their limbs rotated inward, they wreak havoc upon the knee and its support structure. But performed properly (from the hip joints) and achieved gradually, turn-out (along with other dance skills) can make a major contribution to the gymnast's flexibility and strength.

Furthermore, turn-out not only provides greater freedom of movement in every direction but is a valuable tool in landings as well. With proper turn-out, many would-be ankle sprains resulting from low tumbling or dismount landings can be prevented. If the feet are parallel upon a low landing, there is more stress placed on the ankle. But when legs and feet are turned out upon landing, ankles are less likely to turn under. It also becomes easier to stick landings with proper turn-out because the gymnast's base is broader than it would be with the feet parallel.

Summary

Certainly, there are countless other ways, in addition to those mentioned in this chapter, in which dance training can help prevent injury and improve a gymnast's overall performance. Simply put, dance training enhances awareness of the body's mechanics, its capabilities and limitations, and the beauty and excitement that can be derived from the healthful and skillful use of the human body.

In essence, given the nature of gymnastics today, participants must understand that the sport they've chosen consists, to a large extent, of the art of dance. Therefore, gymnastic training should include time set aside specifically for dance instruction. Most importantly, young people about to enter into the sport should be made fully aware that dance and dance training will be a major part of it. To those who are presently involved in gymnastics, dance training can only improve upon what they already know. Coaches and dance instructors also must do everything within their power to make dance enjoyable for the gymnasts because the time gymnasts devote to enhancing their skills through dance technique will be time well spent.

Chapter 2

Ballet and Gymnastics

© Dave Black

Ballet is the dance technique most commonly taught to gymnasts. This chapter will first delve further into the reasons why, as well as looking briefly at the technique's historical origins. The section that is likely to be of the greatest benefit to gymnasts, their coaches, and dance instructors is the one defining more than three dozen ballet terms and their application in gymnastics. These terms have been divided into four subsections: (a) basic body positions, (b) ballet exercises, (c) compulsory ballet steps, and (d) optional ballet steps. Within the sections the terms have been listed, not alphabetically, but *progressively*, according to amount of use by the gymnast as well as degree of difficulty. The compulsory ballet steps are listed in the order in which they appear in compulsory routines, beginning with Class V beam routines.

The Role of Ballet

In the last chapter I talked about the importance of such basics as correct body alignment, the *plié* and *relevé*, use of hands and arms, spotting, and other techniques that can be drawn from the study of ballet. In this chapter, it will become evident that gymnasts can further enhance their performance beyond using these dance fundamentals. The discipline of studying ballet can familiarize gymnasts with the flow that should connect a series of movements. Similarly, ballet training provides gymnasts with self-confidence and a physical awareness known as stage presence—that invisible force that causes all eyes to focus upon a performer. Even if the basics were the only benefits derived by gymnasts, they would be enough to deem ballet training a necessity.

Furthermore, the great majority of dance skills classified as difficulty elements in gymnastics are taken from the ballet repertoire. This technique is also essential to the learning of compulsory dance steps. Gymnasts need technical instruction in pirouettes, *tour jetés*, *fouettés*, and the like.

For all of these reasons, *if* it is only possible for one dance technique to be taught at a gym, that technique should be ballet, and it should be taught by a qualified instructor.

Historical Origins

Ballet, as it is known today, actually dates back to the year 1672, when King Louis XIV established a dancing school in order to train performers for the opera-ballets, the latest events in his new theaters. It was the first time that professional artists were allowed to perform what had previously been considered the "noble dances." Nine years later, the first ballerinas (women who were to dance professionally) took to the stage, and a systematic technique began to form.

Today there are three different schools of ballet technique: the French method (dating back to King Louis XIV); the Russian school (deriving its technique from the French but gaining international respect of its own in the nineteenth century); and the Italian school, better known as the Cecchetti method (named for the man who brought it to Russia in 1874). Within these schools, there are certain poses and movements performed in different ways, and different names given to steps and positions that are actually quite similar. All three share the same basic principles, however, and a dance teacher is likely to use a combination of techniques when developing her or his own method.

Ballet, then, is certainly the oldest of the three dance styles discussed in this book and probably the most widely known throughout the world. Its methods, in fact, have made a significant contribution to both modern dance and jazz, and it is the dance technique most frequently taught in gyms.

Ballet Terminology and Its Application to Gymnastics

I have selected the terms listed in this section from the hundreds that comprise the technique of ballet. Those appearing in this book have a particular relevance to gymnastics.

Basic Body Positions

The body positions listed are basic positions with which all gymnasts should be familiar. Not included in this first section are those body positions that are required as part of compulsory routines (such as *arabesque* and *attitude*). Compulsory movements and poses derived from ballet are defined separately.

Turn-out.   This is the term given to the rotation of the legs and feet, ideally to a 90-degree position. It was established in order to provide dancers with freedom of movement in all directions.

In Gymnastics: As mentioned in chapter 1, it is important for gymnasts to rotate the legs from the hip joints. If they leave the upper leg facing front and attempt to turn out the feet and lower legs only, they will place unnecessary strain on the feet and knees. Dance instructors and coaches, therefore, must be alert to this problem and assist in correcting it as soon as possible. The rotation must begin at the hip and carry down through the feet but should not be greater than the capability of the gymnast!

Positions of the Feet.   Standard to all three schools of ballet, there are five basic positions of the feet, and every step begins and ends in one of them. All of those described below are executed with the feet and legs turned out.

- First position: The heels touch each other and, with perfect 90-degree turn-out, the feet ideally form a horizontal line (see Figure 2.1a).
- Second position: The feet are in the same line as above, but the heels are separated by the length of a bit more than a human foot (see Figure 2.1b).
- Third position: Often omitted by ballet teachers, third position requires that one foot be placed in front of the other, with heels touching the middle of the opposite foot (see Figure 2.1c).
- Fourth position: There are two ways in which fourth position is commonly performed. One is to hold the feet as in third position but with one foot in front of the other and separated by the length of a foot (see Figure 2.1d). Alternatively, feet may

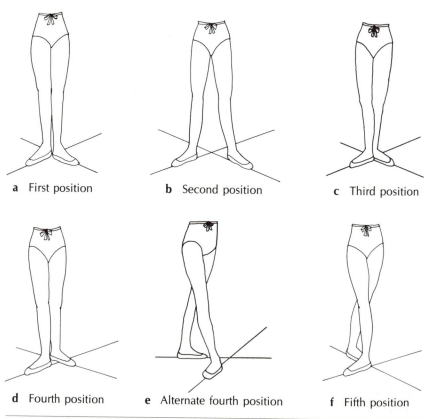

a   First position   b   Second position   c   Third position

d   Fourth position   e   Alternate fourth position   f   Fifth position

Figure 2.1a-f   Positions of the feet

be separated as above but in fifth position (see Figure 2.1e). The choice is generally left up to the ballet teacher.

- Fifth position: The feet are crossed, with the heel of the front foot touching the big toe of the back foot, and the heel of the back foot touching the small toe of the front foot (see Figure 2.1f). (This is also done with 90-degree turn-out.)

In Gymnastics: Gymnasts should perform exercises at the barre or ''in center'' (away from the barre) with at least four of the five positions of the feet. Each requires a different distribution of the body's weight, and, consequently, moving through the various positions will enhance concentration and awareness of body alignment.

Sur le Cou-de-pied. This translates into ''on the neck of the foot.'' The neck of the foot is considered to be between the base of the calf and the beginning of the ankle. Standing *sur le cou-de-pied*, the dancer places the foot of the working leg, toes pointed, at the ankle of the support leg. The dancer bends the knee of the working leg, which is turned out, and holds the foot to the front or the back of the ankle on the support leg. In the Russian method, there is also a low conditional position, which has the small toe of the working foot touching the top of the slipper on the support foot and is always done in *relevé*; and a high conditional position, used for pirouettes, in which the pointed toe is placed halfway up the shin bone.

In Gymnastics: Any of these positions could be used in gymnastics, whether for pirouettes, poses, or any movement requiring a fixed position of the leg. In gymnastics, it's sometimes hard to know what to do with a free leg. If gymnasts want to use *sur le cou-de-pied* as it is used in ballet, they must point the toes strongly and turn out the free leg so that the knee is facing away from the support leg. Hips must remain squared to the direction faced. The gymnast also has the option of using *sur le cou-de-pied* with both legs in a parallel position. If so, the toes of the free foot must still be strongly pointed but placed to the side of the top of the ankle, and both legs must actually be parallel.

Retiré. This word means ''withdrawn.'' In dance, *retiré* is the position in which the thigh is lifted and turned out, with the knee sharply bent and the pointed toes placed to the side (see Figure 2.2), front or back of the supporting knee. This position is also used frequently for pirouettes.

Figure 2.2 *Retiré* to the side

In Gymnastics: Gymnasts may find this a more natural position than *sur le cou-de-pied*. It can also be a very attractive leg position when performed correctly, with the free leg turned out and the hips squared. Although the thigh is raised, the hip must not be. Gymnasts must also be careful not to rest the foot on the supporting knee; they must lightly place toes only at the chosen spot. Again, in gymnastics, *retiré* may also be parallel, with the big toe of the free foot placed to the side of the supporting knee.

Positions of the Arms. Each of the three schools of ballet has its own set of arm positions. Although some of the positions overlap from one school to another, those described and illustrated here are generally the most accepted by ballet schools in this country.

- First position: The arms are rounded and held to the front of the body, with fingertips almost touching. Palms face the body and are in line with the fork of the ribs (see Figure 2.3a).
- Second position: The arms are held to the sides—slightly in front of the shoulders—with as much length as possible while still maintaining a slight curve. The purpose of the curve is to give the illusion of depth from a front view. The elbow is a bit lower than the shoulder, and the wrist a bit lower than the elbow (the elbow should be facing the back and not the floor or ceiling). The hand is also slightly curved, with the palm facing the front of the body (see Figure 2.3b).
- Third position: The third position of the French school is most commonly used. One arm is curved above the head, as in fifth position high, with the other held to the side (second position)

(see Figure 2.3c). It is easily remembered by the calculation, five minus two equals three.

- Fourth positions: The French school also gives us the most commonly accepted fourth position of the arms. Gymnasts can use the calculation, five minus one equals four, to recall that one arm should be held above the head in fifth high, with the second arm curved in front of the body, as in first position (see Figure 2.3d).
- Fifth position low: The arms are rounded and held low in front of the body, with fingertips an inch or two from touching (see Figure 2.3e).
- Fifth position high: The arms form a circle above and slightly in front of the head, so that the fingertips, which are almost touching, are just within the line of vision (see Figure 2.3f).

In Gymnastics: Gymnasts who practice these arm positions will learn how to gain control of their arms and to coordinate varied and interesting arm positions with the positions and movements of their legs and bodies. Carriage and control of the upper torso will also be improved.

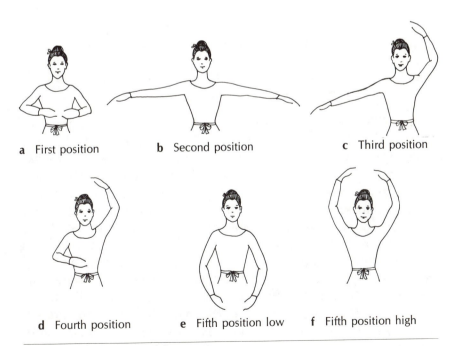

a First position   b Second position   c Third position

d Fourth position   e Fifth position low   f Fifth position high

Figure 2.3a-f Positions of the arms

Extension.   Extension describes the dancer's ability to lift and hold an extended leg in the air. If the dancer, when doing a *développé* to second position, can raise and keep the leg above shoulder level, that is considered good extension.

In Gymnastics: Good extension should be the goal of every gymnast. When displaying good extension, the gymnast will also be showing evidence of strength, flexibility, and bodily control. In addition, such extension will contribute to good balance, whether on floor or beam.

Positions of the Head.   The Cecchetti method designates five basic positions of the head: (a) head erect, (b) head inclined to one side (can be either side), (c) head turned to one side (again either side), (d) head raised, and (e) head lowered.

In Gymnastics: As mentioned in chapter 1, if a gymnast makes little use of the head during routines, he or she will likely hold it stiff and erect throughout. If, however, these five positions are incorporated regularly into dance training, gymnasts will begin to feel comfortable with moving the head. Good coordination is also enhanced by learning to move heads, arms, and legs concurrently.

Ballet Warm-Up Exercises

The following ballet exercises should be performed as often as possible during dance warm-up.

Plié.   This is simply a bending of the knees performed at the barre or in the center, with the feet in any one of the five ballet positions. (Third position, however, is quite often omitted.) The two principal types of *plié* are (a) *demi-plié*, a half bending of the knees, in which the heels always remain on the floor; and (b) *grand plié*, in which the knees are bent until the thighs are horizontal. Except in second position, the heels must rise from the floor when a dancer performs a *grand plié*. With all *pliés*, the movement should be smooth, with the body lowering and rising at the same tempo. Legs must be well turned out, knees remaining over the toes and hips over the heels, and the body's weight must be evenly distributed over all ten toes and the backs of the heels. In ballet, this exercise is performed in order to increase flexibility in joints, muscles, and tendons, and to help develop balance.

In Gymnastics: Whether performed as a warm-up exercise for the benefits cited above, or for the sake of injury prevention (as mentioned in the last chapter), the *plié* should be as much a part of the gymnast's life as it is of a dancer's. The *demi-plié* is the beginning and ending of every jump or leap; and there is no better exercise for experiencing proper body alignment. However, the *grand plié* should not be practiced because it places unnecessary strain on the knees.

Relevé.   The *relevé* is a rise onto the ball of the foot (*demi-pointe*) or onto the tips of the toes (*sur le pointes*). It may be performed either on one foot or on both, and either smoothly, as defined by the French school, or with a slight spring, as required by the Cecchetti method.

In Gymnastics: Gymnasts are expected to rise only to the balls of the feet and will most often execute a *relevé* smoothly. When in *relevé*, weight must be evenly distributed over all five toes; and the ankle must remain in line with the leg. Performed as part of a dance warm-up, at the barre or in center, *relevés* are an excellent exercise in balance and will help provide gymnasts with a feel for the use of the whole foot. The ability to isolate the parts of the foot (toe, ball, heel) is necessary for springing from the floor with the greatest possible elevation and for landing both solidly and with the least amount of strain to the body.

Battement Tendu.   This exercise is commonly called just *tendu* and is performed with the feet in either first or fifth position. The dancer

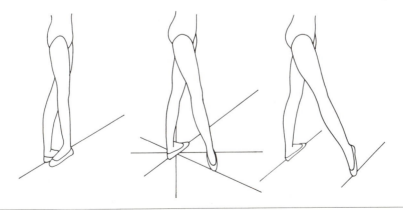

Figure 2.4 *Battement tendu* to the front from fifth position

slides the working foot along the floor (to the front, side, or back), toes first, until the leg is stretched and the knee is straight (the toes are strongly pointed, with the heel raised and foot arched) (see Figure 2.4). When this occurs, the dancer returns the foot to its original position, again sliding the toe along the floor (the heel is not lowered until the very end of the movement). A *tendu* may be performed with the supporting leg either straight or in *demi-plié*, and it is the movement that precedes and finishes every *grand battement* (described under "Compulsory Ballet Steps"). In dance warm-ups, *tendus* are normally performed prior to *dégagés* (see below), both of which are followed by *grand battements*.

In Gymnastics: *Tendus* are excellent for developing turn-out of the leg and foot, particularly when performed to the front and back, where the temptation is to move the hip along with the working foot. In addition, *tendus* assist in developing the instep of the foot and help ensure the correct execution of *grand battements*. As mentioned above, *tendus* should precede *dégagés* in the dance warm-up.

Battement Dégagé.   The *battement dégagé* is performed with the feet in either first or fifth position. The dancer slides the working leg quickly along the floor (as in a *tendu*, to the front, side, or back), lifts it approximately four inches into the air, and then slides it quickly back to its original position. The toes must be strongly pointed while the foot is in the air. These are generally called *dégagés*.

In Gymnastics: Performed either at the barre or in the center of the floor, *dégagés* are part of a warm-up in every ballet class and in many jazz and modern classes as well. They help develop the instep of the foot, increase the ankle joint's flexibility, and enhance awareness of the proper use of turn-out. They are also extremely beneficial in promoting the automatic pointing of toes that must take place whenever a foot rises from the floor. For these reasons, *dégagés* are of tremendous value to gymnasts.

Fondu.   This word means "sinking down" and is basically a *plié* performed on one leg only. For instance, while at the barre, the support leg can *fondu* while the working leg performs a *tendu*. The term can also be used to describe the ending of a movement when the working leg returns to the ground softly and gradually, as in a *jeté fondu*.

In Gymnastics: In general, a *fondu* will offer gymnasts the same benefits as does a *plié*. It increases flexibility in joints, muscles, and tendons and helps develop balance. When practiced regularly, along with *pliés*, the *fondu* provides even more opportunity for the gymnast to become comfortable with the bending of the knee, which is necessary to injury prevention.

Port de Bras.   Translated, this term means "carriage of the arms." But, in ballet, it can mean either the passage of the arms through various positions, or a set of exercises intended to enhance graceful arm movements. The Cecchetti method details eight different exercises for *port de bras*. In ballet classes, however, the exercises most commonly performed at the barre are the forward and the backward *port de bras*.

In the forward *port de bras*, the dancer stands with one arm resting lightly on the barre and the other in second position. The dancer lifts the upper torso and then bends slowly forward at the waist, until standing nose to knees. Meanwhile, the dancer has also slowly lowered the extended arm to the front of the feet. At this point, both the upper torso and the arm reach forward and then begin a smooth ascent, with the arm carrying through both first position and fifth high, and opening once again to second.

In the backward *port de bras*, the arm descends from second position to fifth low. Then, as the upper torso lifts and bends to the back, the arm rises through first position and into fifth high. Here the dancer lifts and lengthens the body as much as possible, with the arch occurring, not in the lower back, but across the shoulder blades.

In Gymnastics: Because gymnasts need to display strength in the use and control of arms, exercises for *port de bras* are essential. The two described above may be performed with the feet in any of the ballet positions, at a barre or in the center. Also, because exercises for *port de bras* can be endlessly varied, dance instructors can design their own, according to the needs of their gymnasts.

Rond de Jambe.   A circular movement of the leg, *rond de jambe* is executed either by the entire leg or from the knee. There are many variations of *rond de jambe*, and it may be performed in either a clockwise or a counterclockwise direction, on the ground or in the air.

In Gymnastics: There are two *rond de jambe* exercises that are valuable for acquiring strength and balance and learning to keep the hips squared while maintaining turn-out. The first is a movement in which a straight leg draws a circle on the floor with the toes, moving from first position to the front, side, back, and returning to first (or in the opposite direction). The second exercise is a circling of the leg from the knee, in which the leg is turned out and raised, with the knee bent, so that the toes are resting lightly at the inside of the opposite knee at the beginning and conclusion of each circle. The gymnast should imagine a piece of chalk attached to the big toe, which draws a perfect circle in the air with each *rond de jambe*. Both of these exercises are best performed at a barre until the gymnasts have acquired the necessary strength and balance to perform it in the center of the floor.

Temps Lié.   This translates into "connected movement." In ballet, it is an exercise consisting of a series of arm movements and steps that flow, either to the front or to the back, through fourth, fifth, and second positions. The key word here is *flow*.

In Gymnastics: The instructor can design for gymnasts any series of movements fitting the above description, beginning with simpler patterns and advancing to the more complex. Some examples follow:

- A simple pattern would be merely to move feet and arms from one position to another, with one leg only as the working leg and the arms and feet always in a corresponding position. For example, with both arms and feet beginning in fourth position, the students would transfer arms and the working foot to fifth position and then to second, repeating this pattern as many times as the instructor has designated.
- A more challenging variation of the above would be to reverse the pattern and to use both legs as working legs. In other words, the students would begin in second position (with both feet and arms), transfer to fifth, with the right foot closing behind, and then to fourth, with the left foot moving forward.
- *Temps lié* can also be done with *développé*, pirouettes, or both. For instance, the students could add a pirouette or *développé* between each of the positions. Alternatively, they could begin in second, pirouette and close in fifth, *développé* into fourth, and then pirouette back into second, and so on.

These exercises are very beneficial in developing the smooth, controlled movements required in transmitting the body's weight from one position to another. Because the *demi-plié* plays a major role in the shifting of weight, gymnasts will also be gaining additional practice with that valuable movement.

Changement de Pieds.   This term means "change of feet" and is commonly abbreviated to *changement*. Standing in fifth, the dancer springs lightly into the air, bringing front foot to the back (and vice versa), thereby landing in fifth position with the opposite foot in front. This is usually repeated several times, in rapid succession, as part of the jumps that often end ballet class.

   In Gymnastics: Whether performed at the end of a warm-up or the end of a class, this exercise is also quite helpful in developing turn-out. As with any series of jumps, *changement* will teach gymnasts to spring into the air, using feet and legs only. Although only in the air momentarily, the toes must be pointed while off the ground. Heels must come all the way down upon landing.

Grand Changement de Pieds.   Translated, this means a "large change of feet." It entails a deeper *plié* and a much greater push from the floor than does the above step. The intention is to stay as little time as possible on the ground and as long as possible in the air.

   In Gymnastics: Naturally, *grand changement de pieds* requires greater leg strength and springing ability than does a normal *changement de pieds*. Gymnasts, therefore, would do well to master both of these steps.

Centre Practice.   This is the name used to describe exercises performed in the center of the room without the aid of a barre. The exercises may be the same or similar to those performed at the barre but are more difficult to perform without support.

   In Gymnastics: Unfortunately, many gyms are not equipped with barres; so gymnasts must often perform balletic warm-ups in the center of the floor, never having had the advantage of the barre's support. However, Gail Grant (1982) says that center practice is "invaluable for obtaining good balance and control" (p. 29). So it is certainly to the gymnast's advantage to perform ballet exercises without a barre than not to perform them at all.

En Croix.   This translates into "in the shape of a cross" and refers to exercises, such as *tendus* or *battements*, that are performed alternately to the front, side, back, and side. For example, performed *en croix*, a *tendu* on the right leg would be executed to the front, right, back, and right, with the entire series then repeated as many times as the instructor designated.

In Gymnastics: When working with *tendus, dégagés,* and *battements,* in particular, dance instructors should always ask gymnasts to perform these movements *en croix*. This will allow the gymnasts to experience fourth position front, second position, and fourth position back, including the feel of turn-out in each of these three positions.

Compulsory Ballet Steps

The following movements are typically required within compulsory routines.

Grand Battement.   This is actually just a large kick that can be executed to the front, side, or back (see Figure 2.5). Although it may seem simple, it requires a great deal of control to perform a *grand battement* while the rest of the body remains still. The upper torso must remain erect and not collapse toward the kicking leg. Hips must remain squared in the direction faced (i.e., the lower torso must not twist with one hip moving forward); and both hips should remain level, even at the height of the kick. The dancer also needs control to keep both knees perfectly straight. Finally, because the accent is on the downward movement of the leg, care must be taken to return the working foot exactly to its original position and no further.

In Gymnastics: Because of the discipline required, *grand battements* make a valuable contribution to a gymnast's dance warm-up. In addition, they can help teach gymnasts a great deal about keeping the hips squared. Finally, because of the frequent use of *battements* in floor and beam routines (often called high forward kicks), gymnasts should take the time to learn how to perform them correctly.

Assemblé.   This step requires that the working foot slide along the floor and then be swept into the air. As this happens, the support leg pushes off the floor and joins (assembles with) the working leg, toes extended. Both legs land at the same time (see Figure

Figure 2.5 *Grand battements* to the front, side and back

2.6). A dancer can perform an *assemblé* with a turn or to the front, side, or back.

In Gymnastics: Executed in its simplest form, this step is found in many of the latest compulsory floor and beam routines. Correct execution of the *assemblé* requires that the gymnast maintain straight legs and an erect upper torso throughout the movement. In movements such as these, the gymnast should always imagine that a string extends from the ceiling, attaches to the top of the head, and keeps the upper torso lifted at all times.

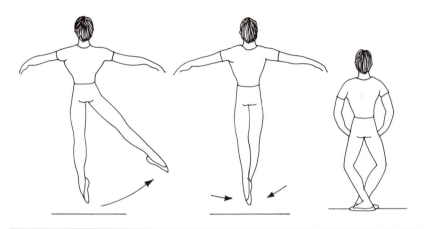

Figure 2.6 *Assemblé*

Sissone.   With a few exceptions, this is a jump initiated from two feet and landed on one. It may be performed in any direction. In ballet, there are literally dozens of variations on the *sissone*.

In Gymnastics: The most common *sissone* in gymnastics is one in which the gymnast begins with both feet together, leaps forward, and lands in *arabesque* (see Figure 2.7). The *arabesque* is described later in this section. This *sissone* is a required movement in many of the latest compulsory beam routines. However, gymnasts should also practice *sissones* to the side, facing both directions. A *sissone* to the side not only provides additional training in springing from the floor, but also might be a valuable addition to an optional routine. If executed on beam, where the gymnast cannot see the

Figure 2.7 *Sissone*

intended direction, and if landed solidly, this is an effective movement. In any *sissone*, the spring should come equally from both feet, and the legs should be fully extended while in the air. The upper torso must remain erect throughout, even upon landing.

Chassé.   This step is similar to a gallop, in that one foot always leads and the other chases (see Figure 2.8). *Chassés* may be performed to the front, side, or back and are generally performed in a series.

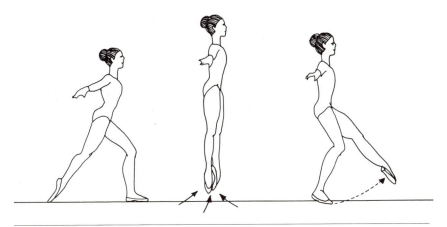

Figure 2.8 *Chassé*

In Gymnastics: The term is used to describe the above movement, generally executed to the front. Performed commonly as part of both floor and beam routines, *chassés* should glide smoothly. At that moment when the back foot catches up to the front foot, the feet spring lightly into the air, with toes strongly pointed and the legs pressed together, before the entire movement is repeated. Because *chassés* are relatively easy to perform, executing them across the floor offers gymnasts the opportunity to experiment with and perfect corresponding movements of the arms.

Pirouette.   To pirouette is to whirl or spin on one foot in *relevé*. Pirouettes require maximum control and balance, and a preparation that involves a solid *demi-plié* and positioning of the arms. Both supply the motive power behind every pirouette. Spotting, which is a requirement for all turns, is of particular importance in pirouettes. The head is the last body part to move as the body turns, yet is the first part to return to the original position. The dancer turns out and bends the raised leg at the knee, holding the toe to the inside of the support leg, anywhere from the ankle to the knee (from *sur le cou-de-pied* to *retiré*). The body should be tilted slightly forward, rather than being completely vertical, with the weight over the ball of the support foot. Multiple pirouettes (doubles, triples, etc.) may be performed, with the heel of the supporting foot remaining raised until the turns are completed. Pirouettes may be performed either inward (toward the support leg) or outward (away from the support leg).

In Gymnastics: Unlike the ballerina, the gymnast is not required to bend her raised leg, with the toe held to the inside of the support leg. Often, the gymnast extends the raised leg and holds it to the back throughout the turn. Pirouettes (even single ones) provide excellent practice in balance, spotting, and control of the arms and torso. Double and triple pirouettes are considered difficulty elements, and gymnasts should have considerable practice with *relevés* and spotting before attempting to execute them. With such practice, gymnasts are likely to have acquired a feel for supporting weight over the ball of the foot and for the balance and spatial orientation spotting can provide. Proper body alignment is yet another major factor in performing a pirouette. If gymnasts are to perform pirouettes successfully, they must keep their shoulders directly in line with the hips, and their hips over the supporting foot.

Pas de Chat.   This term translates into "cat's step," and it is the *pas de chat* from the Ceccheti method that is most well known. The dancer begins in fifth position, with the right foot back. She then lifts the right foot to *retiré* at the side of the left knee. The dancer *pliés* and pushes off the floor with the left leg, which moves diagonally to the side as she then raises it to the inside of the right knee. She makes the landing on the right foot, which is followed almost immediately by the left, which, in turn, closes in fifth position front.

In Gymnastics: Known as a cat leap, the *pas de chat* has undergone a bit of a transformation for gymnastics. Here the step is almost always performed in a forward direction, but the greatest modification is in the movement itself. Although the legs must still be turned out, the feet are not brought alternately to the sides of

Figure 2.9 Cat leap

the knees. Rather, the working leg swings up and forward in a bent position, followed by a swinging forward of the support leg, which passes the descending working leg. The legs follow one another in landing in *demi-plié* (see Figure 2.9). The gymnast must be careful not to lean the upper torso forward as the legs are raised. Finally, if the legs are not well turned out this step will resemble a poorly executed hitch kick (see chapter 3).

Jeté.   Although there are numerous kinds of *jetés*, all are essentially leaps from one leg to the other that may be performed in all directions. In ballet, with *grand jeté en avant* (large leap forward) it is necessary for the dancer to assume only a pose such as *attitude* or *arabesque* while in the air.

<u>In Gymnastics:</u>   A basic *jeté* would be a stride leap in gymnastics, with a split leap fitting the description of a *grand jeté en avant*. The lift of the back leg should be equal to that of the forward leg, resulting in a good split. A split leap is usually preceded by a run or a slide, followed by a solid *demi-plié*. Throughout the leap, the gymnast must keep the upper torso erect, legs turned out, shoulders relaxed, and arms controlled regardless of their positions. The landing is in *demi-plié*, with the rear leg still extended. With a basic *jeté*, the gymnast has much freedom in choice of leg, arm, and body positions. They may bend, twist, or arch, as long as the movements and landing are controlled.

Arabesque.   The basic position of the body, performed in profile, is a support on one leg, with the other leg extended to the back, at a right angle to the body and support leg (see last pose of Figure 2.7). The latter can be straight or in *demi-plié,* and the arms are extended, in any combination, above the head or to the front, side, or back, creating as long a line as possible from fingertips to toes. Shoulders must be square to the direction being faced. The three schools of ballet use a wide variety of *arabesque* positions, all of which follow these general guidelines.

In Gymnastics: There is greater freedom allowed in the position when used in gymnastics. *Arabesque* need not always be in profile, and the body can twist, as can legs and arms. An *arabesque penchée,* which is a leaning *arabesque* in ballet, is a front scale in gymnastics. The upper body, in other words, is lowered as the working leg is raised still higher. If the gymnast continued to raise the working leg to a perfect standing split, the final position would then be a needle scale.

Passé.   This word means "passed." In ballet, it is generally the knee of the supporting leg that is passed by the foot of the working leg when the dancer is moving from one position to another. For example, in *développé passé en avant,* the dancer draws the foot of the working leg up the side of the support leg to the knee. Upon reaching the knee, the working leg is then fully extended to the front of the body. *Passé* can also refer to the passing of legs in the air or the movement in which one foot is lifted and passes either in front or in back of the supporting leg.

In Gymnastics: The term *passé* is often incorrectly used to define both the actual *passé* and the *retiré* (see "Basic Body Positions"). These terms are not interchangeable, however, as *passé* is a *movement* in which the knee is passed, and *retiré* is a static position in which the foot of the working leg is placed at the supporting knee. Therefore, when a routine calls for gymnasts to pass a bent leg through a *passé* position, that is actually what is meant by *passé.* But when gymnasts are required to strike a *passé* pose, they are technically being asked to pose in *retiré.*

Chaines.   Translated, this word means "chains" or "links." In dance, it stands for a series of quick turns that are linked together. *Chaines* are performed in *relevé,* either on pointe or on the balls of the feet, in a straight line or in a circle.

In Gymnastics: *Chaînés* are best learned a half-turn at a time, with the legs turned out, feet in *relevé* in first position, and the arms alternately opening and closing (moving from second to first position) with each half-turn. Gymnasts should perform *chaînés* on the balls of the feet.

These are best practiced on a straight line marked by chalk or masking tape or a joint in the floor mat. Standing on the line, as described above, the gymnast should look over the right shoulder (if turning to the right) at a fixed spot. Then, pivoting toward the right on the right foot, the eyes maintain contact with the spot for as long as possible, until the head must finally whip around, completing the turn ahead of the body. In a half-turn, the gymnast will have finished facing in the opposite direction, still on the line, looking over the left shoulder. The feet remain in turned-out first throughout, with heels together and legs tight.

Chaînés are an excellent exercise to promote spotting and control of the arms and upper torso. They can also be used quite effectively as connections between dance and/or gymnastic elements. For example, at the conclusion of a tumbling pass, a gymnast might do two *chaîné* turns into the corner, followed by a body wave, two more *chaînés* down the side of the mat, followed by a cartwheel. (The gymnast has to use turns sparingly, of course, or judges will deduct points for repetition.) *Chaînés* might also help the gymnast connect a split leap to a handspring, or a side body wave to a side leap.

Fouetté.   Translated, this word means ''whipped'' and refers to either the whipping of a raised foot past the support foot, or the

Figure 2.10 *Fouetté*

whipping, from one direction to another, of the body. There are a great number of *fouettés* found in ballet, but the most common is probably the *fouetté* turn, technically known as *fouetté rond de jambe en tournant*. The dancer performs a series of rapid turns on one leg that are provided momentum by the whipping action of the working leg.

In Gymnastics: When a gymnast is told to *fouetté*, he or she is usually being asked to perform what is known as a *grand fouetté en tournant*, or a large turning *fouetté* (see Figure 2.10). The gymnast thrusts the working leg forward to hip level, pushes off the support foot, and turns so that the landing occurs on the support foot, with the body facing in the opposition direction from which the movement began. The support leg lands in *demi-plié*, with the working leg held to the back, still at hip level. In ballet, a *relevé* may replace the spring into the air. In gymnastics, however, the latest compulsory floor routines typically call for a *fouetté* that includes the jump.

Gymnasts performing *fouettés* must be sure not to lower the leg prior to completing the movement. In other words, if the leg is initially thrust to hip level (as it should be), it must remain at that height throughout the entire movement. A helpful tool for the gymnast to imagine, once the leg has swung upward, is that the big toe is stuck in a hole in a wall, and it must remain there until the *fouetté* is completed.

Développé.   The dancer slowly draws the working leg up the side of the support leg and extends it to fourth position front, second, or fourth position back. Once the leg is extended, the dancer holds it in the air with perfect control (see Figure 2.11).

Figure 2.11 *Développé*

In Gymnastics: One present compulsory floor routine calls for *développé* walks in which *développés* to a parallel *retiré* are alternated with steps. However, because this movement requires balance, control, and the ability to hold the hips both level and square to the direction being faced, it is an excellent exercise for all gymnasts. If possible, gymnasts should learn the *développé* at a barre rather than without support in the center of the floor so they can acquire the necessary erectness of the torso. If performed with a good extension (see "Basic Body Positions"), a *développé* can also be a most impressive optional movement, particularly when performed on beam.

Attitude.   With the support on one leg, the dancer lifts the other leg to the back, with the knee bent at a 90-degree angle to the body. With the leg well turned out, the knee is higher than the foot. The dancer extends the arm on the side of the support leg to the side, with the other arm curved overhead (see Figure 2.12a). In *attitude croisée devant* (see Figure 2.12b), the dancer holds the bent leg to the front of the body, with the knee pressed outward and the foot as high as possible. In this position, the high arm is on the same side as the support leg.

In Gymnastics: The gymnast is not required to hold the arms as described above while in *attitude*, but must assume the proper

Figure 2.12a *Attitude croisee derriére*

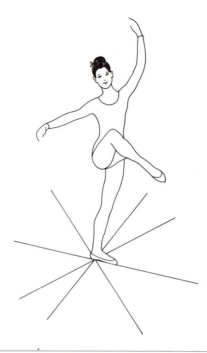

Figure 2.12b   *Attitude croisée devant*

positioning of the working leg. Compulsory routines include both front and back *attitudes*, as well as an *attitude* turn. In optionals, gymnasts can choose from a variety of arm positions while in *attitude*. Possibilities include holding the arms in fifth high or having one arm extended to the front and the other to the side. Two arm positions from ballet that also could work nicely are *demi-bras* and *bras en lyre*. The former is a halfway position of the arms, as they are extended forward at both half the height and half the width of second position. The hands are open and palms slightly forward, giving the impression of asking or reaching for something. *Bras en lyre* means "arms in the shape of a lyre." The arms are held as in fifth position high, but the hands overlap, one above the other. This is an arm position from the French school.

Tour Jeté.   This is the name commonly given to what is technically known as *grand jeté dessus en tournant*. Begun as a *grand jeté*, this leap requires that the body execute a half-turn in midair, legs passing close to one another, and the landing made with the body

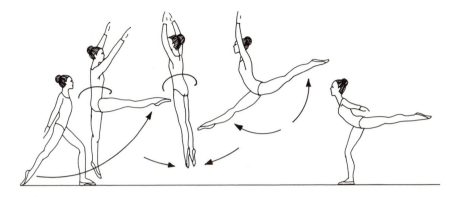

Figure 2.13   *Tour jeté*

facing the direction from which the leap originated. The landing is in *demi-plié,* and in *arabesque* (see Figure 2.13).

In Gymnastics: To perform a *tour jeté* correctly, the knees must be taut and the legs must pass through first position. The best way for gymnasts to avoid bent knees and legs swinging wide is to practice *tour jetés* across the floor in slow motion. In other words, the gymnasts should isolate each movement involved so they can understand that the *tour jeté* is actually comprised of a *grand batte-ment* to the front, a *fouetté,* and a *grand battement* to the back, which remains in *arabesque.* In performance, the gymnast is not required to hold the *arabesque* position upon landing, but may assume it momentarily and then proceed into another movement.

Optional Ballet Steps

The following steps are appropriate for inclusion in optional floor and/or beam routines.

Développé fondu.   In this movement, the support leg sinks in *fondu* as the working leg executes a *développé.* In other words, the dancer slowly draws the foot of the working leg up to the knee of the support leg and then extends it. Meanwhile, the support leg slowly bends.

In Gymnastics: Although a simple movement, a *développé fondu* can be quite effective when performed correctly. It requires balance and control and is a rather nice study in opposition, with one leg sinking and the other extending. The secret is for the movements to take place simultaneously and for the working leg to be raised as high as possible, in contrast to the bent leg. *Développé fondu* may be performed in either turn-out or parallel.

Soubresant. This is a jump that springs from both feet, normally traveling forward, and lands on both feet. From fifth position, the dancer *demi-pliés* and pushes into the air with straight legs and pointed toes, maintaining the crossed feet of fifth position. The dancer then lands simultaneously on both feet, still in fifth position with the same foot front.

In Gymnastics: Gymnasts have the option of performing a *soubresant* in any direction, incorporating any arm positions. Care should be taken to keep the body straight and the legs tightly crossed; upon landing, the buttocks must remain tucked under.

Échappé. This word means "escaping." The step entails moving the legs from a closed to an open position, as in going from first or fifth to second position or from fifth to fourth. In *échappé sauté*, a spring from fifth position finishes opened in *demi-plié*. In *échappé sur les pointes*, the dancer finishes the movement in *relevé*, with the legs straight.

In Gymnastics: In both *échappé sauté* or *échappé sur les pointes* (moving to second or fourth position), the feet must travel an equal distance from the original center of gravity. The upper torso must also stay strongly lifted. Both movements have numerous possibilities for use in optional routines, perhaps especially on beam. A gymnast could spring from first to second *relevé*, for instance, pivot on the balls of the feet to face the end of the beam, lower heels and legs to a lunge position, and then execute a pirouette.

Detourné. This is a pivot turn on two feet in *relevé*. The dancer begins with one foot in front and reverses the position of the feet as the turn is completed. In a *demi-detourné*, the dancer executes a half-turn toward the back foot. The heels are then lowered, and the back foot becomes the front foot.

In Gymnastics: The *demi-detourné* can be especially useful in changing direction on the balance beam, and comes in handy when a gymnast is looking for a small, less common turn. The gymnast can use any variety of arm movements to add interest to the step, including moving the arms from fifth low, through first, and into fifth high; or slowly opening from fifth high to second. In order to be effective, however, the gymnast must accomplish these turns with good balance, straight legs, and a lengthened torso.

Glissade.   With this step, the dancer must *demi-plié* in fifth position and then glide the working foot along the floor to a strong extension a few inches above the floor. The other foot pushes off the floor so that, for just a moment, both legs are straight. The dancer then shifts the weight to the working leg in *fondu* and slides the other foot, which is still raised a few inches off the floor, into fifth position in *demi-plié*. *Glissades* may or may not include a change of feet and must begin and end with a *demi-plié*.

In Gymnastics: Because gymnasts can execute *glissades* in any direction, they're perfect as traveling steps, either on floor or beam. In ballet, they are used to link other steps, and gymnasts might also find them particularly helpful in that way. For example, on beam, a gymnast might perform a *soubresant* and a *glissade*, both traveling forward, followed by a *demi-detourné* to change direction, *développé* to the front, and into a back walkover. *Glissade* means "glide," and that's exactly what the movement should do. From *demi-plié* to *demi-plié*, the movement should flow.

Chaînés Papillon.   This step is so named because the *chaînés* must be performed "like a butterfly." The arms, then, are responsible for this task. The dancer begins the series of *chaînés* with the arms held in second position. Taking a step on one foot, the dancer lowers the arm on that same side and raises the other arm. The arm movement is then reversed as the dancer executes the second half of the turn.

In Gymnastics: This variation on *chaînés* makes a lovely addition to any optional routine. The gymnast should first be capable of performing ordinary *chaînés* before attempting to coordinate these arm movements. Finally, if the motion is to resemble that of a butterfly, the arms must flow softly as they're raised and lowered.

Balancé.   *Balancé* is a rocking step in which the weight is shifted from one foot to the other. For example, from fifth position with the right foot in front, the dancer *pliés*, *dégagés* the right foot to the side, and lands on it lightly in *plié*, crossing the left foot either in back or in front of the right ankle. The dancer then steps in *relevé* onto the left foot, lifting the right foot slightly off the floor, only to step back onto the right foot in *plié*, with the left *sur le cou-de-pied*. The dancer repeats the entire movement to the left side.

In Gymnastics: Performed smoothly to counts of three, the *balancé* is a very pretty step. With hands on hips or perhaps arms folded across the chest, it can even be reminiscent of folk dance and used accordingly with the appropriate music. The head can also make a contribution, rocking side to side (ear to shoulder) with the rocking of the movement. Regardless of what the head and arms are doing, though, the legs must be well turned out—with the hips squared—if the *balancé* is to be attractive.

Cabriole.   With this movement, the dancer kicks the working leg into the air, followed by the second leg, which beats against the first (from beneath it), sending it even higher (a double beat may also be executed). The dancer then lands on the lower leg. *Cabrioles* may be performed to the front, side, or back.

In Gymnastics: This dance step would certainly make a valuable contribution to a gymnastics routine, particularly if performed on beam. In a forward *cabriole*, the chest must not collapse toward the legs. In a *cabriole* to the side, the body should be in a straight line, from head to feet, just as the beat occurs at the height of the movement.

Tour en l'air.   This is a turn in the air in which the dancer pushes straight into the air from *demi-plié*, executes a 360-degree (or 720-degree) turn, and lands in fifth position with the opposite foot in front. Dancers use spotting, as in pirouettes; and they also assist the movement with their arms. Although this originally was a turn performed only by male dancers, many choreographers now require females to execute it as well.

In Gymnastics: This advanced dance step requires much training before it can be executed properly and safely. First, the gymnast must be capable of attaining the height necessary for completing a turn in the air. Second, the gymnast must be able to leave the ground and return to it in a straight line. A common cause of injury is landing off-center from such a turn. However, the gymnast who does master the *tour en l'air* will have a powerful tool to use in optional routines. Once learned, the *tour en l'air* can also be landed in a number of interesting ways, such as in a large second position or on one knee.

Summary

With the exception of a few advanced steps, most of the terms described above would normally be studied in the first two years of ballet training. That means, considering the requirements and challenges of competitive gymnastics, that all of the terms deserve serious consideration by the serious gymnast. Dance instructors, coaches, and gymnasts may use the terminology section as a reference source. Gymnasts need to be familiar with those steps that are part of their compulsory routines. They should also become familiar with all of the basic body positions and use the ballet exercises to acquire the ability and finesse to perform the compulsory movements. Finally, the section on optional ballet steps is a good starting point for gymnasts who are looking for movements to include in optional routines.

Chapter 3

Jazz Dance and Gymnastics

© Dave Black

With all of the many benefits derived from the study of ballet, why would gymnasts require additional training in jazz dance—particularly when their time is already so limited? That is a question asked by many coaches and by gymnasts themselves. This chapter, therefore, attempts to answer that question, pointing out the many valuable functions of jazz dance. It will first cover descriptions of body part isolations, which play a great role in jazz dance and can be of such help to gymnasts. It then provides descriptions of a number of movements common to jazz dance, listed separately under headings for compulsory and optional movements, as many of these are now required steps in compulsory routines.

Two critical points must be made initially that should encourage the reader to give serious consideration to the information contained in this chapter. The first is that not every body—nor personality—is balletically inclined. The second is that jazz dance has recently begun playing a more prominent role in gymnastics, as evidenced by the number of steps derived from jazz that are now compulsory movements.

The Role of Jazz Dance

The characteristics that Dolores Kirton Cayou (1971) uses to describe traditional African dance also point out the basic differences between jazz dance and ballet. They are as follows:

1. the use of bent knees, with the body close to the earth—excluding those times, of course, when the dancer is jumping;
2. the tendency to use the foot as a whole in that the weight is shifted immediately from one foot to the other;
3. the isolation of body parts in movement, such as the head, shoulders, hips, rib cage, etc.;
4. the use of rhythmically complex and syncopated movement;
5. carrying as many as two or three rhythms in the body at once—polyrhythm;
6. combining music and dance as a single expression, one feeding the other;
7. individualism of style within a group style; and
8. functionalism—becoming what you dance—the art of real life (p. 4).

There are some fundamental differences between jazz and ballet that concern the gymnast. The most obvious is that, whereas ballet tends to concentrate on body *lines*, jazz masters the art of individualizing *parts*—heads, shoulders, hips, and rib cages, in particular. Jazz is also about energy. At those times when a soft, rounded look to the arms and hands is inappropriate, jazz training shows itself in the energy surging through the arms and to the fingertips. At the other end of the body, jazz dance provides gymnasts with a better feel for the use of the entire foot, resulting in greater spring and an enhanced ability for sensing the balance beam.

The element of rhythm is yet another major consideration and an area in which vast differences exist between jazz and ballet. Jazz dance emphasizes the rhythms of the body as well as the rhythms of music. Although the flow developed by ballet is certainly critical, it's equally important to perfect a sense of timing and phrasing. Without it there can be no fluency. Without fluency, a composition can give the impression of a string of pearls, minus the string!

Finally, there is what Cayou (1971) refers to as "individualism of style." Whereas ballet tends to stress conformity, jazz encourages technical ability for the sake of self-expression. Training gymnasts in jazz dance, therefore, can be of great help to the coach who wishes to bring out the individual styles and personalities of his or her team members.

For those gymnasts wishing to make use of this technique in optional routines, there are numerous musical styles and tempos that lend themselves to a swing of the hips, a shake of the shoulders, or a toss of the head. These movements can add flair to a routine and contribute greatly to the expression of a gymnast's personality, even when the routine is performed without music, as on beam. For those whose personal styles rule out such movement, the value of isolating body parts and experiencing new rhythms lies in the resulting control and awareness. Thus heads, shoulders, hips, and rib cages should be technically mastered even by the most *classical* of gymnasts.

Historical Origins

What is jazz dance? The question may seem straightforward, but it has actually been the cause of some controversy. According to Marshall and Jean Stearns (1968), authors of *Jazz Dance, the Story of American Vernacular Dance,* it is American dancing that has its roots in Africa. However, it is "vernacular" in that it is "native and homegrown" and is limited to dancing performed strictly to the rhythms of jazz music. It is their belief that instructors teaching "modern jazz dance" are teaching a combination of European and American styles, which have little to do with jazz (p. xiv). They further contend that today's theatrical dancing is a blending of vernacular and artistic dance, with its origins in modern dance and ballet.

Dolores Kirton Cayou (1971), the author of *Modern Jazz Dance,* defines that term as "a continuing evolution of jazz-oriented dance" (p. 13). She states that it is an expression of the African culture that simply did not exist for many people until it had gained white acceptance and appeared on stage during the 1920s. At that time, tap dance (a major part of American vernacular dance) became quite popular with white people; and it was probably then that the term jazz dance came into being. Cayou states, however, that jazz dance "is *not* limited to the social or stage dances of the 1920s. The definition of jazz dance must include the entire dance culture, or the term has little meaning" (p. 11).

Selected Common Jazz Movements

Unlike that of ballet, the technique of jazz dance does not have a specific terminology because it has not codified positions and movements. There are, however, certain steps that are common to jazz dance. Although many steps and movements do overlap from one technique to another, those mentioned in this chapter tend to be found more frequently within the context of jazz.

The following terms are divided into three sections to provide easy access for the reader. The first section describes common isolations. Used in relation to jazz dance, the word *isolation* refers to the movement of one body part, separate from the rest of the body, which may be either still or moving in a different way. The technique is fundamental to jazz dance and of infinite value to gymnasts. Even though it is likely to be a part of the lesson plans of any teacher providing jazz instruction, it warrants specific attention here because of its significance.

The second section describes those movements common to jazz dance that are found in the most recent compulsory routines. They are listed in the order in which they appear in compulsories, beginning with Class V beam routines.

Lastly, while not found in present compulsory floor and beam routines, the steps and movements listed as ''optional'' are also quite common to jazz dance. They may prove suitable for inclusion in certain optional routines and have much to offer as part of the gymnasts' dance classes. In addition to incorporating them into warm-ups and exercises performed across the floor, the dance instructor should consider including these movements in combinations choreographed for the gymnasts to perform in class. They are listed in general order of difficulty.

Isolations

There are two basic ways in which body parts can be isolated. They can move either smoothly, as in a circling of the hips, or sharply, as in a sudden turn of the head. The body parts commonly isolated in jazz dance are the head, shoulders, hips, and rib cage (presented in order of difficulty).

The following are some essential isolation exercises that should be included in every gymnast's dance instruction. Although the majority of attention will be focused on the moving part, the gymnast must remember to control the rest of the body and to hold it in a properly aligned position. The basic stance for each of these exercises, therefore, is in parallel first (feet straight and no more than six inches apart), body erect, shoulders relaxed and down, and arms held at the sides and slightly away from the torso.

Head Isolations.   Even a subtle head movement can be extremely effective as an accent or a transition between movements. Gymnasts should practice the following head actions to increase control and body awareness.

Front and Back.   With the rest of the body remaining completely still, the head drops forward (chin to chest) and back (as far as it can comfortably go). A common tendency is for the shoulders to rise, so the gymnast must concentrate on keeping them relaxed. The easiest way to learn this exercise is to perform it in a continuous motion from front to back. Once the gymnasts feel comfortable with this, they can add a stop in the middle (front-center-back-center). The movement should be sharply punctuated.

Side-to-Side.   Both this and the following exercise are best learned with a continuous motion. The student tilts the head from one side to the other and brings the ear as close to the shoulder as possible. The shoulder does *not* come up to meet the ear. The student must also be sure to keep the head squared to the front. In other words, the head does not turn or twist at all as it drops first to one side and then to the other. When the gymnasts have mastered this, they again add a stop in the center and perform the movement (both down and up) as sharply as possible.

Looking Side-to-Side.   With the head remaining perfectly level, the gymnast turns to look over one shoulder and then the other. Once the stop at center is included, it's important for the gymnasts to focus the eyes every time they return the head to center. Therefore, spotting something at eye level can be very helpful.

Head Rolls.   The student normally begins with the head forward (chin to chest) and then rotates it in the direction and at the tempo called for by the instructor. It is important for the student not to cut off the roll to the back by circling toward one shoulder and then lifting the head across the middle to the other shoulder. Although the head must remain as light as possible to avoid unnecessary tension in the neck, it should make a complete circle. The instructor begins with circles that take an entire eight counts to complete (the head will be forward on "one" and "eight" and toward the back on "four") and works in both directions. When the count is abbreviated to four, the teacher should be sure that the movement continues to be smooth, as students have a tendency to change to a staccatolike motion on a four-count. (These are, however, head *rolls*.) Finally, with the count reduced to two, the gymnast swings the head sharply toward the back and lets it swing quickly around to the other side, using momentum to keep the movement going.

Head Swings.   The gymnast drops one ear to the shoulder and swings the head from side to side, chin to chest. Once this has become a familiar movement, the instructor can combine the swings with a head roll. If beginning with the head tilted left, the exercise calls for the student to swing right, swing left, swing right and all the way around, ending with the head tilted right. The swing, in other words, would be 1/2, 1/2, 1 and 1/2.

Shoulder Isolations.   The following exercises involve the shoulders only. Although the arms must move a little, gymnasts will have to concentrate to keep them as still as possible.

Up and Down.   Everyone is familiar with shrugging, and the simplest shoulder isolation is the one in which both shoulders are lifted to the ears and then dropped. Following this, the gymnasts are asked to lift just one shoulder, and then to lift one shoulder at a time, in alternation.

Forward and Backward.   With arms at their sides, students move both shoulders to the front and back. Once this is a comfortable movement, they follow the same progression outlined in the previous exercise.

Shoulder Circles.   Still with their arms at their sides, gymnasts will circle, first both shoulders and then one shoulder, to the back. The shoulders, in other words, must move forward, up, back, and down. A more difficult exercise involves circling to the front (back, up, forward, and down).

Shimmy.   At this point, students raise their arms to second position. (In jazz, arms are not rounded in second, but strongly extended, with the elbows slightly bent and lowered. Palms are flat and facing front, with fingers extended and separate from one another.) The gymnasts push one shoulder forward at a time, imagining they're to strike something in the space directly in front of that shoulder. If students are having a hard time keeping the entire arm from moving forward, they should further imagine that they are holding on to something stationary (such as a floor-to-ceiling pole) while attempting to move the shoulder only. The exercise is begun slowly, alternating shoulders. As the students become more adept, the count is quickened until, finally, they are performing a shimmy. (Instructors must allow several weeks for students to learn this.)

Hip Isolations.   With hip isolation, the knees must be bent to allow the pelvic girdle its pendular motion. The feet must be planted firmly on the floor to minimize leg movement.

Side-to-Side.   In this first exercise, the students stand in parallel first and in *plié* and swing the hips from side to side (like a pendulum). Students must remember that this is a hip isolation and that the upper torso must not move!

Front-to-Back.   This is the same as the side-to-side exercise, except that the hips push alternately forward and backward. There's often a bit more temptation here to include the upper torso and shoulders in a contractionlike movement, so instructors should be attentive to this problem and correct it immediately.

Hip Circles.   Once familiar with swinging the hips side to side and front to back, the gymnasts can be asked to perform hip circles in both directions (as with the head rolls, the circles must be complete).

Figure Eights.   This is definitely the most difficult of the hip isolations mentioned here. The gymnasts must imagine that their hips are drawing figure eights on the floor below them, but these figure eights are lying on their sides (not standing upright as the number eight would). The hip is lifted to one side and forward, circled to the back, then lifted across to the other side, and so forth.

Rib Cage Isolations.   The following rib cage exercises are very difficult. They require a lot of practice, body awareness, and control.

Side-to-Side.   With this exercise, the gymnast must imagine that the rib cage is a cardboard box. In order to isolate the rib cage from side to side, the gymnast must lift that box from where it is sitting and slide it sideways onto a shelf. This particular isolation is normally easier if first performed with a stop at center, rather than continuously from side to side. In other words, the ribs are lifted, slid to the side, then brought back to the center and relaxed. The movement is then repeated to the other side. Once the students have mastered this, they can try it with a continuous motion; but the temptation is quite strong to move the hips simultaneously.

Front-to-Back.   Some students find this a more natural, and therefore easier, motion. The rib cage is lifted and then simply pressed forward (with the shoulders moving slightly to the back) and backward, creating a slight contraction in the upper torso. This, too, is normally less difficult when performed with a stop at center. But there's an even greater tendency to include the hips with this isolation.

Circling.   Once the students have gained control over this particular area of the body, they can move on to circling the rib cage in both directions. By that time they will be quite adept at controlling, directing, and isolating all of the above body parts.

Compulsory Jazz Movements

Compulsory floor and beam events now show greater use of such jazz movements as the following. This could indicate a new direction for gymnastics.

Figure 3.1 Side body wave

Side Body Wave. This movement is similar to a forward or backward body wave (described below) in that the motion is continuous and fluid. The gymnast lifts the shoulder, rib cage, arm, and hip on one side consecutively, followed immediately by the same parts on the other side, so that the result is smooth and wavelike (see Figure 3.1). The gymnast should keep the feet planted and resist the temptation to include the head in the sideward motion. Unlike in a forward or backward body wave, the head is not part of the movement in a side body wave and should remain fairly erect throughout.

Tuck Jump. This is a jump straight into the air from both feet, with the legs tucked under the body (they're lifted and sharply bent at the height of the jump, as illustrated in Figure 3.2). The legs are then straightened and the landing made in *demi-plié*, on both feet. One variation of this, found in compulsories, is a tuck jump in which the gymnast also performs a 180-degree turn. The gymnast should not round the back, as in a contraction, but should keep it straight throughout.

Body Wave. Although contractions are crucial to the success of proper body waves and are a major part of modern dance, body waves themselves are practiced and performed regularly as part

Figure 3.2 Tuck jump

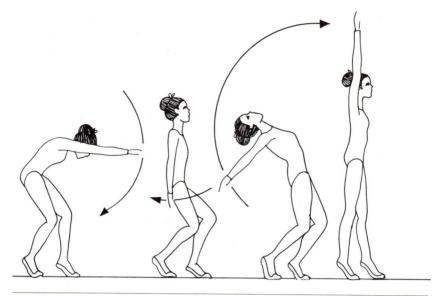

Figure 3.3 Body wave

of jazz dance. They are, in fact, evidence of the fluidity and bodily control that help comprise jazz.

The forward body wave is perhaps the most common (see Figure 3.3). In this movement, the body begins in a semisquat position. The knees, hips, abdomen, and chest (in that order) push forward and upward in a fluid, wavelike action, with the arms normally flowing to the back. The head, initially lowered to the chest, completes the wave by lifting, dropping slightly to the back, and ultimately returning upright.

Because there are so many bodily areas involved, this movement is often easier to learn when one area is eliminated. This is accomplished by practicing the body wave while kneeling on the floor. The knees, therefore, are not included, and the gymnast has a stable base upon which to experiment with the feel of the wave, using only hips, upper torso, and head. As illustrated in Figure 3.4, the

Figure 3.4 Exercise for learning body wave

gymnast begins by sitting back, with legs folded under and hands grasping the ankles. The gymnast then uses the arms to help push the hips up and forward, as the back arches and head drops to the rear. The motion proceeds to reverse itself, without a break in the flow, until the gymnast has resumed the original position. However, to experience the full effect, the gymnast should perform several such body waves, one flowing into another. (The order of body parts, in both the forward and backward motion, is hips, abdomen, chest, head.)

Lunge.   Lunges are certainly among the most common movements in compulsory routines, particularly on beam. Gymnasts are required to perform both small and large lunges, to the front, side, and back, with legs parallel and turned out. Lunges can initiate and finish a turn, lead into a *grand battement*, precede a forward roll, or connect steps in any number of other ways. A lunge, essentially, is no more than a *plié* (*demi-* or *grand*) on one leg, with the other leg extended in the opposite direction. For instance, in a forward lunge, the forward leg is bent and the other leg extended to the rear. In a sideward lunge, if the right leg is bent, the left leg is extended to the left. Regardless of the type of lunge, however, there are some common elements that gymnasts should keep in mind. Perhaps the most important is the fact that, as with any *plié*, the body must not give the impression of sinking. Rather, as the knee bends, the upper torso must make an extra effort to stay lifted, contrasting with the lowering of the bent leg. Further contrast should also be evidenced between the leg in *plié* and the extended leg. Therefore, the gymnast must be sure the extended leg is perfectly straight with the toes strongly pointed. As with any *plié*, whether performed in parallel or turn-out, the bent knee must be pressed directly over the toes.

Straddle Jump.   In this spring from both feet, the legs are extended into a straddle at the height of the jump, prior to closing, straightening, and landing. The gymnast must take particular care to keep knees straight and toes pointed and must also concentrate on keeping the back straight, as it's easier to perform this with the upper torso leaning forward. In compulsory routines, gymnasts are required to extend the arms either straight to the front or straight to the sides. If using this jump in optionals, a gymnast might choose to lift the arms over the head in a "V" or to push the arms, with either hands pointed or palms flattened toward the floor, between the legs at the height of the jump.

Stag Jump.   The gymnast jumps straight into the air, assuming a stag position: forward leg bent at the knee and rear leg extended to the back. In a single stag, there should be a striking contrast between the bent and the extended legs. The head should remain erect and focused at eye-level, and the extension of the arms should assist in the elevation of the jump (see Figure 3.5).

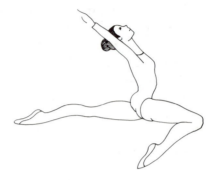

Figure 3.5   Stag jump

Fan Kick.   In an outward fan kick (the most commonly performed), the leg kicks to the front of the opposite foot and then continues to swing up and outward from the body (in the shape of a fan). It is usually completed with the foot of the working leg closing in first or in fifth position back. As simple as this may seem, it is a most unnatural movement for some students. Legs, after all, don't often swing away from the body, and because they have a lot more experience swinging in the other direction (as when crossing a leg or mounting a bicycle), there is a tendency for some gymnasts to perform the fan kick in the opposite direction. Frequent practice, however, can cure that tendency without much difficulty. To avoid a sinking in of the body as the leg is kicked, the gymnast should maintain an erect position throughout, with buttocks tucked under and only the leg doing all of the apparent work.

The fan kick lends itself to a number of possible variations, including the fan turn. In that movement, the gymnast executes a quarter-turn simultaneously with the fan kick.

Stag Leap.   A leap is the equivalent of a *jeté* in ballet (and a split leap the same as a *grand jeté*). A stag leap, though it ends as a *jeté*, is more common to jazz. The gymnast lifts the working leg high, with the knee sharply bent as the body rises from the floor. The support leg lifts and stretches to the back. Finally, prior to landing, the gymnast extends the forward leg to *jeté*. This is similar to a stag jump except that the stag leap moves forward. Variations include the extension of both legs to a split leap (a stag split leap is found in several of the most recent compulsory routines) or a twisting of the hips to the side. In all of these leaps the head should face forward and the eyes should be focused at eye level.

Stretch Jump.   The gymnast pushes off both feet, extending the arms above the head, and lengthening the body as much as possible. In compulsories, a 180-degree stretch jump is required in which the gymnast performs a half-turn while in the air. It is necessary, therefore, to attain enough elevation to complete the turn cleanly. With good extension of the arms, body, legs, and feet, the gymnast should give the longest possible impression at the height of the jump. The gymnast should also lengthen the neck, holding the head erect, in order to contribute to this impression.

Hitch Kick.   Also known as a scissors kick, the hitch kick may be executed to the front or back, but is most often performed forward (see Figure 3.6). The gymnast kicks the working leg as high as possible, immediately pushing off the support foot and thrusting that leg upward as well, so that it passes the working leg in

Figure 3.6 Hitchkick

its descent. The gymnast makes the landing in *demi-plié*, on the first leg. The second leg remains high upon landing, and the body must remain erect throughout—particularly upon completion of the step, where there is a tendency to sit into the landing. It is also essential that the gymnast control the arms throughout the movement to keep them from flapping.

Side Leap.   The gymnast begins by facing forward, but executes a quarter-turn as the working leg kicks up and to the side. The gymnast then pushes off the support foot, also lifting that leg to the side. Both legs must be equal in height when the leap is at its peak. The landing is in *demi-plié*, on the working leg, which remains turned out (see Figure 3.7). The head must remain erect, and the arms must be extended to the side and controlled throughout the movement. With perfect extension of the legs, feet, and arms, the gymnast will give the widest possible impression at the peak of the leap.

Figure 3.7   Side leap

Optional Jazz Movements

There are many beginning and advanced jazz movements suitable for inclusion in optional routines.

Seat Spin.   Sitting on the floor with knees tucked into the chest, the performer propels this spin with the hands. It is necessary to lean in the direction of the turn and allow both head and shoulders to turn as well. The back should stay straight, toes pointed, and body securely tucked throughout the turn. Variations include extending one leg straight to the front, or extending both legs straight up, as in a V-sit.

Knee Spin.   Knee spins, whether they involve one knee or an alternation from one knee to the other, have made a comeback in today's theatrical dancing. The performer can drop into a knee spin from a standing position, rise out of a knee spin to a standing position, or simply initiate it while kneeling. Gymnasts should be aware that knee pads are critical if the spins are not being practiced or performed on a cushioned floor mat. The spins require an erect upper torso, steady arms, and spotting of the eyes, even if the gymnast is only executing one turn.

Body Arch.   Like the tuck and the stag, the arched position is used often in jazz. One very effective use of the arch is that which takes place on the floor. From a sitting position, with one leg straight, one leg bent, and one hand supporting the body, the gymnast pushes the hips and chest upward. The back arches, the head drops to the rear, and the working arm can extend upward, backward, or to the side. The extended arm and leg should remain perfectly straight, in contrast to the arch of the back, for this movement to be completely effective. The eyes should focus on the ceiling and not roll to the back of the head.

Kick-Ball-Change.   This step may be performed either in place or as a small traveling step. Despite the fact that it is comprised of three movements, the kick-ball-change is performed to two counts and counted ''one-and-two.'' The accent is on the ''one'' and ''two,'' as the ''and'' is a very subtle movement. If beginning on the right, the performer would kick the right foot forward in what might be described as a *quick flick* (this is a small forward kick that takes place from the knee). The performer then brings the ball of the right foot down to the back, shifts the weight momentarily onto it, and then moves fully onto the left foot. The movement, then, is just exactly as it is described by its name, with the *change* indicating a change in weight from the *ball* of the other foot. If performing more than one kick-ball-change, the gymnast repeats the movement on the same side, as the legs do not alternate. It is also important to realize that the leg movement essentially takes place directly under the body. Kick-ball-change is a quick movement, and there is simply not enough time for the performer to attempt either a large kick or a large backward step.

Backward Scale.   Unlike the forward scale (or *arabesque*), a scale to the back is seldom seen in ballet. In jazz, this movement is generally referred to as a back lay-out. An arch is required as the gymnast bends back toward the support leg and raises the free leg as high to the front as possible (see Figure 3.8). With this movement, too, the extended limbs must remain straight and the eyes focused on the ceiling. The backward scale requires a good deal of balance and should not be attempted, particularly on beam, if it can't be executed without wobbles.

Figure 3.8   Backward scale

Hecht Jump.   Known also as an arch jump, this is a jump in which the arms swing forward and upward as the body lifts from the ground and the back arches. With the back arched, the feet and head incline toward the back and the hips and chest are pushed forward. The toes must be strongly pointed and energy evident through the extension of the fingertips while the body is in the air. The body and legs straighten quickly, just prior to landing.

Step-Slide.   Known also as a jazz slide, this movement has a couple of variations that are seen often in jazz dance and tap. In the first variation, the performer takes a step to one side, finishing in a lunge position, with the second leg straight and its foot being slid along the floor. The dancer or gymnast actually begins the slide before the first foot completely reaches the floor and extends the arms out to the sides to assist the gliding movement. If two or more slides are performed consecutively, the second leg continues to move toward the first, eventually crossing in front of it, so that the movement can begin again.

Figure 3.9 Step-slide

In the second variation of the step-slide, the gymnast kicks the free leg, and the slide actually occurs on the support leg (see Figure 3.9). The gymnast crosses one foot in front of the other, placing the body's weight upon the forward foot and kicking the other leg high and either to the side or to the front. As the leg is kicking, the gymnast must lean backward, extend arms high to the sides, and slightly lift the weight from the support foot, allowing the slide.

Split Jump.   The gymnast springs straight into the air with both feet, attaining enough height to assume a full split before bringing the legs back together and landing in either *demi-plié* or a squat position. The same elements that are critical to a well-executed straddle jump must be given consideration here.

Ring Leap.   This is executed in the same manner as a split leap, except that the rear leg is bent upward, toward the head. The head, in turn, tilts toward the rear, with the back slightly arched. The forward leg should be fully extended and the toes on both feet strongly pointed. The gymnast should be careful to *arch* the back as opposed to *leaning* back. The body straightens prior to landing (see Figure 3.10).

Illusion Turn.   This movement, which is frequently seen in ice skating, can be extremely effective when used in dance or gymnastics. It is a turn on one leg, with the body bent forward (nose

Figure 3.10   Ring leap

to knee) and the working leg raised to a split position. The gymnast begins the movement by simultaneously lowering the upper torso and raising the free leg to the back, followed immediately with a turn, which takes place on the support leg. As the turn is completed, the gymnast raises the upper body, with the free leg remaining high but now to the front (see Figure 3.11). The most

Figure 3.11   Illusion turn

important factor is that the movement be continuous and swift so that the illusion can take place.

Switch-Leg Leap.   Gymnasts use this leap frequently in optionals, but they must execute it well in order to receive the proper credit from judges. The leap is begun as a *jeté* in which one leg kicks up and forward and the second pushes from the floor and rises to the height of the first. Although it isn't necessary at this point for the legs to attain a full split, they must do so when they are quickly switched and then separated once again. Landing will take place on the original support leg. As in any leap, the arms can help to attain greater elevation if they are fully extended and not raised above shoulder level. The shoulders, in turn, must remain lowered and not hunched toward the ears. The head is erect and the eyes focused forward. The hips should stay squared toward the direction faced throughout the leap.

Summary

There are hundreds of other steps and movements that have originated from jazz dance, including the jazz walk and jazz run, body rolls, turns, flat-back, and triplets. In addition, there are warm-up exercises that can be used to promote flexibility, rhythm, and the precise use of the body and its parts. Jazz is beginning to play a greater role in gymnastics—from compulsory routines to optional routines. Therefore, gymnasts will find that including jazz as part of dance training will be tremendously beneficial.

Chapter 4

© Jack Adams

Movement Education and Gymnastics

In the first edition of *Judging and Coaching Women's Gymnastics*, Bowers, Fie, Kjeldsen, and Schmid (1972) wrote,

> There has been a paradox in the use of dance with other elements in gymnastic routines. The number of creative combinations is infinite, but this has not insured originality. The gymnast has great freedom for creativity in movement, yet on the whole, gymnastics has used only a select group of dance movements.

Few would dispute the importance of creativity and originality, whether it be in the use of dance with gymnastics or in the composition of an optional routine. Yet judges do tend to see very little of either during the course of a meet. If this is to change, individuality must become the goal of every gymnast.

But how does the gymnast work toward the development of individuality when there are so many skills to be learned? How does a coach prevent team members from becoming mere imitations of one another? All gymnasts possess unique personalities, but are they able to communicate those personalities to an audience while performing routines?

Naturally, the most logical solution is to begin striving for creativity while the gymnast is very young—preferably at the preschool age. This is the time at which self-consciousness can be nipped in the bud and self-expression can easily be taught through movement education. Movement education offers numerous benefits to both experienced and budding gymnasts. Modern dance (covered in chapter 5) serves many of the same purposes as movement education, and may be most appropriate for those very experienced gymnasts who may feel uncomfortable with some creative aspects of movement education.

The Role of Movement Education

Movement education has many benefits for those who experience it. Some benefits, like the development of poise, coordination, and physical fitness, can also.be garnered from lessons in tumbling and other skills-acquisition programs. The acquisition of skills, however, does not necessarily enhance creativity and self-expression.

Movement education promotes these traits because it uses a problem-solving or a *guided discovery* approach to instruction. The teacher does not conduct a lesson in movement education with the same methods that he or she would use to teach a class emphasizing skills acquisition. In other words, the instructor does not stand before the class and demonstrate, with the students' response being mere imitation. Rather, the instructor presents *challenges* to the children, such as ''Show me how small you can become,'' or ''Show me how slowly a turtle moves.'' It is then the students' responsibility to find their own solutions to the problem.

Because there is no right or wrong response to such challenges, the children discover the unlimited number of movement possibilities and learn that there is generally more than one solution to any problem. They become better able to *imagine*—to see beyond what already exists. That, in turn, results in *creative* solutions to challenges.

Furthermore, because a problem-solving approach to instruction leaves little room for error, every student has the opportunity to experience success often. A successful child is a self-confident child who learns to trust his or her individuality.

Historical Origins

There is some confusion and a bit of controversy with regard to the use of the term *movement education*. There are those who use it as an alternate term for *movement exploration*, those who think the latter should be used only in relation to method and not content, and those who define movement education as an approach to teaching motor skills that incorporates both content and method.

At any rate, it is generally agreed that movement education has continuously evolved since its beginnings in England in the 1930s, when Rudolf Laban migrated from Germany. Laban had spent a number of years studying movement in both drama and dance, and he developed a system of analyzing movement through the elements he referred to as time, weight, space, and flow. He also believed that *experimentation* should be used as a teaching method.

When Laban began his work in England, elementary classroom teachers were generally conducting their own lessons in physical education. These lessons were based on recommendations contained in a government publication entitled *Syllabus of Physical Training for Schools*, and they consisted of exercises that were usually performed in unison, following the teacher's demonstrations. These exercises gave little regard to the children's differences.

Laban's work began receiving attention, particularly from women, as he and his followers conducted courses in modern dance. Many men were skeptical due to their training in physical education and Laban's association with dance. However, gradually his methods extended to Western Europe and have been increasingly accepted in the United States as well.

Over the last 15 years, movement education has developed into a significant part of the elementary physical education curriculum in this country. It has also become familiar to classroom teachers and to many other professionals working with children, and it is frequently offered in college preparation programs.

According to John S. Fowler (1981), in his book entitled *Movement Education*, "This acceptance has been facilitated by a better understanding on the part of teachers of the underlying structure of movement education and of the needs of children and the goals of education and learning'' (p. 10).

Exploring Movement

Movement exploration is often used to describe method, as opposed to content. In essence, it is no more and no less than experimentation with the body and its capacity for movement. For the purposes of this book (i.e., the encouragement of the gymnasts' creativity and self-expression), movement exploration will be used (as opposed to *movement education*) to define an approach to teaching movement skills, games, and dance as they apply to the gymnasts' needs.

With movement exploration, locomotor, nonlocomotor, and manipulative skills are not merely learned in a technical way, but explored in every way possible. In an article entitled ''Movement Exploration,'' Elizabeth Halsey and Lorena Porter (1970) wrote the following:

> [Movement exploration] should follow such basic procedures as: 1) setting the problem; 2) experimentation by the children; 3) observation and evaluation; 4) additional practice using points gained from evaluation. Answers to the problems, of course, are in movements rather than words. The movements will differ as individual children find the answer valid for each. The teacher does not demonstrate, encourage imitation, nor require any one best answer. Thus the children are not afraid to be different, and the teacher feels free to let them progress in their own way, each at his own rate. The result is a class atmosphere in which imagination has free play; invention becomes active and varied. (p. 76)

This success-oriented philosophy, therefore, dictates that instructors never publicly criticize students for incorrect responses. If a group has been challenged to skip, but one child hops instead, that child should not be pointed out. Rather, the instructor can ask for a demonstration by someone who was skipping correctly. The instructor can also use verbalization in such a situation by describing the differences between skipping and hopping. He or she then reissues the challenge. If the same child still responds incorrectly, the instructor is alerted to an area in which that child requires attention. However, the instructor should offer the attention at times when it's possible to provide it privately and positively.

Basically, there are three ways to explore movement with a problem-solving manner of instruction. Instructors can use the elements of movement, imagery, or music to guide students to a discovery of the unlimited number of movement possibilities.

The Elements of Movement

What is movement? What does it consist of? How best can movement possibilities be explored so that variety and originality are demonstrated? For the gymnast's purposes—particularly the gymnast who will eventually perform optional routines—the elements of movement provide the most significant answers to these questions because they provide the gymnast with alternative ways of performing the locomotor and nonlocomotor skills comprising the routines.

The first step in this process is for the gymnast to grasp the meaning of these elements. Thus it is the dance instructor's responsibility to incorporate exploration through the elements of movement into the lesson plans. Such exploration will include a review of movements in terms of space, shape, force, flow, time, and rhythm. For example, if the locomotor skill of walking were being explored, the student would have a number of choices with regard to *how* to perform the walking. It could be executed forward, backward, to the side, or possibly in a circle (the element of *space*). The walk could be performed with arms or head held in a variety of positions (*shape*), heavily or lightly (*force*), with interruptions (*flow*), quickly or slowly (*time*), or to altering rhythms (*rhythm*). Each of the six movement elements is described below.

Space.   The element of space is broken down into two components. The first, personal space, is the area immediately surrounding the body. It includes whatever can be reached while remaining in one spot. The rest is referred to as general space and is normally limited only by floors, walls, and ceilings.

Both general and personal space consist of three levels. When standing upright, one is at the middle level. Anything lower to the ground than that is considered the low level. Positions or movements performed in *relevé* or in the air take place at the high level.

Space also takes into consideration the bodily and spatial directions of forward and backward, and right and left. Finally, movement performed through general space will also involve pathways, which will be straight, curving, or zigzag.

Implications for Gymnastics: When performing optional floor or beam routines, the gymnast is required to make varied and interesting use of the allotted space. On beam, the gymnast must not move back and forth repeatedly across the length of the apparatus. On floor, the gymnast is not permitted to use the same path for each of the three tumbling passes. In general, the gymnast is not allowed to move consistently in the same direction, to stay in one spot for more than a moment or two, or to remain in an upright position throughout.

When choreographing, therefore, the gymnast must determine whether he or she is making any of the above errors. If too much time has been spent at the middle level, perhaps more leaps, hops, or jumps should be included. The gymnast could also experiment with the ways in which the low level could be most effectively used. Would a fall be appropriate? A forward roll into a straddle split? How many ways are there to lower and lift the body, whether it be on a floor mat or on a surface four inches wide? Do all steps move forward? If so, the gymnast must experiment with movements that travel backward, or to the right or left. On floor, what do the pathways consist of? Are they all straight, or do some of them curve and/or zigzag?

Shape.   Modern dancers believe that any bodily shape is appropriate to dance, as long as it amply expresses the conviction of the choreographer. Over the years, this belief has resulted in countless ways to form the human body and its parts. This, then, is the element of shape.

Implications for Gymnastics: Shape (and all other elements) can be explored while performing various locomotor and nonlocomotor skills. I gave the example of changing the shape of the head or arms while walking. The shape of the entire body might also be changed during the walk, with the body being lengthened or shortened or becoming angular or rounded. But shape can also be explored on its own, without the use of locomotor and nonlocomotor activities. The instructor might ask the students to assume a round, flat, wide, narrow, long, or crooked shape. Alternatively, the instructor might ask them to take on the shape of animate or inanimate objects, such as a table, chair, tree, snake, or teapot.

Experience with this element will make it easier for gymnasts to choose poses for beam and floor (opening and finishing poses on floor are especially critical). They are also far more likely to make interesting use of body parts commonly forgotten, such as arms, hands, and head. Through the exploration of shape, gymnasts, like modern dancers, will become capable of performing ordinary locomotor and nonlocomotor activities in less than ordinary ways.

Force.   Force relates to how heavily or how lightly a movement is performed and to the amount of muscle tension involved. Tiptoeing, for instance, requires much less force and muscle tension than does stamping feet. Similarly, moving like a butterfly requires much less force than moving like a tin soldier.

Implications for Gymnastics: If a floor exercise routine is accompanied by music that never varies in its quality of sound, it's likely that the force of the gymnast's movement will also remain unchanging—a serious error from the judges' point of view. But it is on beam, where the gymnast has only motion with which to create an impression, that special consideration must be given to the element of force. The gymnast, therefore, must look carefully at a routine, asking whether or not a variety of both light and heavy movement has been employed by both the body as a whole and the individual parts. Some more forceful movements the gymnast might choose to include would be a *grand battement*, a strong contraction, a punching motion of the hands and arms, a sudden turn of the head, a tuck jump, or a back handspring. Lighter movements might include a side body wave, a *développé*, a *chassé*, a soft circling of the head, or a gentle swing of the hips.

Flow.   The flow of movement is either bound (punctuated or halting) or free (uninterrupted). For example, bound flow would be motion resembling that of a robot, or a series requiring the performer to hop-hop-stop, hop-hop-stop. Free flow is visible in the action of the skater gliding effortlessly across the ice or in the flight of an eagle. Free flow can also be likened to sustained motion (refer to chapter 5, "Qualities of Movement") or to a sentence, which might have a breathing pause but not a complete pause until the end.

Implications for Gymnastics: In gymnastics, the word *flow* generally refers to the way in which one skill connects to the next. The resulting movement, which should more frequently be an example of free flow, unfortunately most often resembles bound flow. Like the sentence cited above, a series of movements on floor or beam may perhaps include a breathing pause but not a complete pause until it's ended. If gymnasts don't have adequate experience with (or a natural tendency toward) the element of flow, they will have trouble connecting their movements smoothly and effortlessly. Thus their "sentences" will be punctuated with needless "commas" and even "semicolons." There is room for both bound and free flow in a routine. For example, when the actual intention is bound flow, as in the staccato movements of a kick-step-punch-punch, the movement should not be smooth. But when the series is *chassé*-pirouette-body wave, the audience should not have time between steps to consider them separately. Rather, the steps should blend one into the other, giving an overall impression of fluidity. Therefore, both types of movement should be evident in any routine. On floor, the flow must generally complement the music. But, on beam, the gymnast has great freedom of choice in how to use this element.

Time. The element of time relates to how slowly or quickly a movement is performed. Because all movement is neither very slow nor very fast, however, it also concerns the range of speed in between. Students might be asked to move as though they were being filmed in slow motion or flitting from flower to flower like a hummingbird. To experience the continuum from slow to fast movement, the instructor might lead the students in movement that begins very slowly, as in a slow-motion walk, and that gradually accelerates until the students are in a full run. This is known as *accelerando*, the reverse of which (from fast to slow) is called *ritardando*.

Implications for Gymnastics: Changes in tempo are a requirement in gymnastic routines. Therefore, it's essential that gymnasts have ample experience and feel comfortable with movement ranging from the very slow to the very fast. They should also be capable of using this element creatively. A run, for instance, needn't always be fast. A sudden drop to the mat or beam, rather than a slow fall, can add an element of surprise to a routine. Briefly alternating quick and slow movements can add both variety and originality, as when a sudden drop is followed by a slow circling of the arms and then a rapid arch of the back and a contraction back to the floor.

Rhythm.   Rhythm, although often associated with the element of time, is mentioned separately here because of its many facets and benefits to gymnasts. This element not only relates to music, but encompasses the many rhythms of life as well. Words, for instance, have rhythm, as do the various locomotor activities (e.g., the rhythm of a hop differs from that of a skip). People, in fact, possess their own personal rhythms for both thinking and functioning. The element of rhythm encompasses all of these aspects.

Implications for Gymnastics: Rhythm is a fundamental part of gymnastics because gymnastics is about movement, and movement is rhythm. To perform efficiently, gymnasts must be at ease with this vital element. They must be well acquainted with the rhythms of walking, skipping, galloping, sliding, and all other forms of physical locomotion. They should feel as comfortable with the rhythms of a waltz as they do with the rhythms of rock and roll (refer to chapter 6, ''Music in the Dance Class''). They should be able to move smoothly from a *fouetté* to a kick-ball-change, and they must be capable of expressing a variety of rhythms with a variety of body parts. The head, for instance, should be as adept at staccatolike movements from side to side as it is at a smooth roll across the chest. The arms should move effortlessly, whether they're performing rapid punches into the air or slow, curving arcs above the head. The shoulders should be as comfortable with the rhythm of a shimmy as they are with the rhythm of a quick shrug.

There is also a rhythm to be found in words, and that particular aspect of rhythm can be of great help in remembering a series of movements or even a single movement. Kick-ball-change, for instance, is performed in the same rhythm in which it is spoken. Mentally hearing the words can train the body to move as it should until, eventually, the movement becomes automatic. Similarly, a gymnast might be better able to recall a combination if he or she committed the relevant words to memory. For example, for a stretch jump followed by a squat and then a forward roll, the gymnast might memorize ''stretch, squat, and forward roll,'' mentally spoken in the same rhythm in which it's to be executed. An alternative for the same pattern might be ''up, down, and forward roll.'' Certain sounds can likewise be helpful in mastering a particularly difficult movement (rat-a-tat-tat for a side-to-side shake of the head that starts on one side and finishes strongly with the head tilted to the other). In addition, gymnasts can use counts such as "one-two-and-three-four" (refer to "Varying Rhythms" in chapter 8). The dance instructor or gymnastics coach, therefore, should be attuned to the needs of the gymnast having trouble with certain movements or patterns and should experiment with these methods until he or she finds one that offers the gymnast a solution.

Exploration Through Imagery

As mentioned earlier, the creative person is one who is better able to *imagine*. Exploring movement through the use of imagery, therefore, is of great significance to enhancing creativity. It is of particular significance in this age of technology, when television, videos, and computers provide children with so many ready-made images.

When using imagery to explore movement, the instructor must keep in mind the age and experience of the students. It's unlikely, for example, that a preschooler could demonstrate anxiety or disillusionment. The image of an elephant is bound to be more familiar to this age group than that of an anteater. Similarly, young students will relate better to the image of a washing machine than they will to that of a food processor.

To cite a specific example of the use of imagery, let's return to the locomotor skill of walking. The instructor could ask the students to walk as though sad, angry, or tired. Alternatively, they could pretend to walk in different environments (e.g., through sticky mud, on the moon and weightless, on a crowded city sidewalk). In addition, the instructor might tell them to walk like the animals or favorite characters (e.g., Santa Claus, the Incredible Hulk, or a circus clown). Similar examples for other locomotor and nonlocomotor skills include the following:

Running:
   Carry a football in the big game.
   Try to catch a bus.
   Run as if you were being chased by somebody.
   Carry something or someone very heavy.
   Dribble a basketball down the court.
   Run the last leg of a long, exhausting race (with the finish line just ahead).

Bending and Stretching:

Stretch to pick fruit from a tall tree.

Flop like a rag doll.

Stretch as though waking up in the morning.

Bend as though tying your shoes.

Stretch to put something on a high shelf.

Bend to pat a cat.

Stretch as though climbing a ladder.

Bend to pick flowers or vegetables from the garden.

Shaking, Wiggling, and Vibrating:

Be a snake.

Be a piece of bacon sizzling in the frying pan.

Be a bowl of Jello (when the bowl is disturbed).

Be a baby's rattle.

Be a leaf in the wind.

Be an electric toothbrush.

Twisting:

Pretend you are the inside of a washing machine.

Act like a screwdriver in somebody's hand.

Twist like a wet dishrag being wrung out.

Twist your foot as if you were stamping out a cigarette.

Striking:

Box with an imaginary opponent.

Beat against a stuck door.

Play a big bass drum.

Swing a bat.

Hammer a nail.

Chop wood.

Swat at a mosquito.

Pushing and Pulling:

Move as though pushing a swing.

Pull a rope in a game of tug-of-war.

Push heavy furniture.
Pull a kite.
Push a lawn mower.
Pull an anchor from the water.
Push a car stuck in snow.
Pull a wagon or sled.
Push a grocery cart.

Moving as Though at Work:
Dig a ditch.
Carry groceries.
Shovel snow.
Sweep the floor.
Rake leaves.
Wash dishes.
Wash windows.
Wash a car.

Exploration With Music

Although it's very important to explore movement on its own, without music, it's not surprising that using music is often the most popular method of exploring movement. Music, after all, is enjoyable and provides an outside source of inspiration. It's also possible for music to provide additional experience with both imagery and the elements of movement. For example, *Flight of the Bumblebee*, by Rimsky-Korsakov, conjures up a very specific image, which results in a certain type of movement. It also offers experience with the movement element of time, as it is a very fast piece of music. In chapter 6, I discuss the use of music in the dance class, placing special emphasis on the necessity for *variety*. Variety in music is also critical in movement exploration if the students are to discover a wide range of movement.

Because students may experience self-consciousness or a lack of confidence when they first begin to work with music and movement exploration, the instructor should refrain from simply playing a song and asking the class to "Move in the way the music makes you feel." A better method would be to begin with an activity like "statues." In this way, the instructor minimizes the students' self-consciousness by introducing them to improvisation to music in the form of a game.

In the game of "statues," the teacher plays a piece of music, starting and stopping it at various, indiscriminate intervals. The students, meanwhile, have been instructed to move in any way they like, as long as there is music playing. As soon as the music stops, however, they must freeze into statues and remain absolutely still until it's resumed. Each time the students repeat this game, the instructor should use dissimilar pieces of music to accustom the gymnasts to moving to a number of different styles. The instructor can make the game more difficult by asking the students to freeze in a particular manner. For instance, they might be required to freeze in a certain shape (e.g., round, crooked, wide, narrow), or in a position that's low, high, balanced on one body part, and so forth. Eventually, the gymnasts will become comfortable with this type of exploration, and thus the game will no longer be necessary.

Establishing Developmental Progressions

As much fun as all of the above may seem, instructors should follow certain principles in the presentation of challenges if the challenges are to be met with enthusiasm and therefore be of benefit to the students. Developmental progressions, for example, are necessary to any program of movement exploration. It's critical that instructors begin with the simplest of skills and images; the challenges must then develop in a logical progression. Otherwise, the students won't feel comfortable with problem-solving, because they won't have progressed through the stages necessary to make them comfortable. Students would obviously explore the locomotor skill of walking, for instance, prior to skipping (with running, jumping, hopping, and galloping leading up to skipping). Similarly, bending and stretching would certainly precede twisting.

In addition, instructors should take into consideration the age and experience of the students with regard to the level of imagery used. Similarly, the steady, pulsing beat of rock and roll would be more likely to inspire an initial response than a polka. Without this basic approach, students will be overwhelmed and become discouraged. The idea is to make them feel good about experiencing movement by starting slowly and providing them with frequent opportunities to experience success. To this end, there are three general progressions that should be kept in mind:

1. Children should work as individuals prior to exploring movement with a partner and, following this, in cooperation with a group.
2. The students must first use the body as a whole. They can later be asked to move both arms and/or both legs together, separate from the rest of the body. Laterality is then introduced, followed by the opposition of body halves. Here students discover, for example, that the lower half of the body can bend while the top half stretches. Finally, body parts are isolated and used individually. Use of parts such as hands and faces can certainly be introduced earlier, but much experience is required before children can comfortably move just head, hips, or shoulders.
3. Generally, children between the ages of three and five would rather pretend to *be* something than pretend to do something. In other words, they would rather pretend to be an airplane than pretend to do the flying of that plane. It is only much later that they can demonstrate how such experiences might *feel*. So, the natural progression is being, doing, and then feeling.

Handling Discipline

Because success is always the goal in a program of movement exploration, atmosphere plays as vital a role as skill progression. Discipline, therefore, must be handled with special care. With so much activity involved, however, maintaining discipline isn't always easy.

One consideration in the instructor's favor is the fact that children like to show off—to display their abilities, *particularly* to their teachers. The instructor can use this to his or her advantage when presenting challenges. If the challenges are introduced with words like ''Show me you can'' or ''Let me see you,'' the children will *want* to show that they can! Furthermore, when a program is

success-oriented, it's likely that there will be fewer discipline problems. After all, when a child is experiencing success, he or she is
less likely to become bored or to want to wreak havoc upon the
class.

There are, however, two important rules that instructors must
explain to the students in the beginning and enforce consistently.
The first is that there are to be *no collisions*. (In fact, there should
be no touching unless it happens to be a specific part of an activity.)
At the start, this may be difficult to enforce, especially with the
youngest students, because they generally enjoy colliding with one
another! So it's the instructor's challenge to make it a goal for the
children *not* to interfere with each other.

The instructor can accomplish this by asking the students to space
themselves evenly at the beginning of every movement session.
He or she should explain the idea of personal space, perhaps by
encouraging the children to imagine they're each surrounded by
a giant bubble: whether standing still or moving, they should avoid
causing any of the bubbles to burst. Another image that works quite
successfully is that of dolphins swimming. Children who've seen
these creatures in action, either at an aquarium or on TV, will be
able to relate to the fact that dolphins swim side by side but never
get close enough to touch one another. The goal, therefore, is for
the students to behave in a similar manner.

The second rule that will contribute to a manageable and pleasant
environment is that there can be no noise. This will ensure that
the instructor's challenges, directions, and follow-up questions can
be heard at all times, with no need for shouting. This is accomplished by the establishment of a signal that indicates it's time to
stop, look, and listen ("Stop, look at me, and listen for my next
challenge"). The instructor must choose a signal that the students
must *watch* for (like two fingers held in the air), or something that
they must *listen* for (like a hand-clap or three taps on a drum). It
should be noted that a whistle is not generally suitable, as it can
be heard above a great deal of noise and possesses certain military
connotations. Nor will the instructor's voice be effective, as it's
heard so often by the students.

In general, as in all matters relating to movement education, a
positive attitude is the key. Movement sessions should take place
in a friendly, encouraging, and fun atmosphere, balanced with
some basic ground rules for human behavior. This atmosphere,

together with the fact that the children are experiencing success, will ensure that discipline problems will be minimal.

Summary

Movement exploration ensures success more often than not and builds confidence in one's individuality. It is additionally beneficial in that gymnasts (of all ages) are instilled with a certainty that any challenge will almost always have more than one response. Therefore, any movement or combination of movements can be executed in any number of ways. Thus when the time comes to find a way to use a certain passage of music, or to make use of the beam at a low level, gymnasts who've experienced movement exploration and problem-solving are far more likely to discover an original and creative solution.

Chapter 5

Modern Dance and Gymnastics

Of the dance techniques covered in this book, modern dance is certainly the most difficult to define, essentially, because it is so all-encompassing. It is probably also the dance technique least often taught in gymnastics centers. The most common technique is ballet, followed by jazz dance, which is gaining in popularity because today's music lends itself primarily to the rhythms of jazz dance. Therefore, coaches are increasingly seeking instructors who can teach jazz to their gymnasts as well as ballet. This chapter, however, will define the ways in which modern dance can—and already does—contribute to gymnastics.

The Role of Modern Dance

Modern dance can best be described by way of a comparison to ballet. Modern dance is a back-to-basics brand of dance technique. While performers of ballet were defying gravity by rising onto their toes, the first modern dancers were casting off shoes in order to move barefoot upon the earth. Ballet is based upon a formal and often difficult technique, but modern dance commonly employs a vocabulary of fundamental locomotor and nonlocomotor skills. Whereas ballet has codified its technique and begins and ends all movement in one of the five positions of the feet, modern dancers believe that there are as many positions as the human body can assume. Ballet strives for lightness and unearthliness; modern dance recognizes the energy and effect derived from the body's contact with the floor. Ballet teaches its students control of the torso with its emphasis on a lengthened and arched spine. Modern dance recognizes the value of a supple spine. Finally, and perhaps most importantly, whereas ballet tends to be an exacting technique, from which the choreographer must design his or her pieces, modern dance is based upon the expression of the choreographer's ideas and emotions, and is designed accordingly—thus improvisation plays a vital role in this dance style.

In general, learning modern dance as well as ballet would contribute to gymnasts' technique by making them more well-rounded. Although ballet has tremendous value to gymnasts and has even contributed certain steps and movements to the gymnastics repertoire, the intention is not to turn gymnasts into ballerinas. Gymnasts need a back-to-basics approach as well as formal technique; they need to discover different bodily shapes, positions, movements, and so on. They certainly must feel comfortable with contact with the floor. Finally, although they have to learn control of the upper torso, they should also possess the flexibility of a supple spine. In short, gymnasts need to experience modern dance.

After providing historical background information, this chapter cites specific benefits of modern dance, placing particular emphasis on the areas in which modern dance can strongly impact gymnastics. They include the basic locomotor skills, nonlocomotor skills, contracting and releasing skills (the concept of a strong and supple spine), and improvisation.

Historical Origins

Less than a century old, modern dance was originally a break from the tradition and formality of ballet. It was ''an expression of the freedom of the spirit'' (Penrod & Plastino, 1980, p. 47), and its early years, not surprisingly, coincided with Prohibition, World War I, and the women's suffrage movement.

Today, because of the cross-fertilization that has taken place between techniques (modern often borrows from the concepts of ballet, as well as from jazz and ethnic dance), it is no longer considered strictly nontraditional. Yet it's still not uncommon to hear it referred to as unorthodox.

Modern dance is undoubtedly unique in that it is the only technique that can trace its history by looking at the works of those who've performed it throughout the years. Although it had begun prior to Isadora Duncan, she is generally considered the "mother of modern dance" because of her success in bringing the new style to widespread audiences. Her contributions include the use of the whole body for movement (as opposed to the balletic emphasis on the legs and feet) and the shedding of shoes and confining ballet costumes.

Those who succeeded Duncan and made their own major contributions include Ruth St. Denis, who found inspiration in the East and the Orient, and Ted Shawn, whose masculine choreography improved the status of the American male dancer. There followed Martha Graham, with her technique of contraction and release, and Doris Humphrey, who believed in the principle of fall and recovery. More recently, the world of modern dance has seen the controversial Merce Cunningham, who choreographs "by chance"; the multimedia approach of Alwin Nikolais; the theatricality of Alvin Ailey; and the strong images and rapid movements of Bella Lewitzky. Finally, there are the names of today—Twyla Tharp, Pilobolus, Jennifer Mueller, Kei Taikei, and Anna Halprin—whose efforts ensure the continual growth and evolution of the definition of modern dance in the future.

Although that definition remains elusive, it can be concluded that modern dance is concerned with life as it is today. It is contemporary, and it will always remain so because the one absolute concerning modern dance is that it is ever-changing.

Locomotor Skills

Modern dance's concern with the basic locomotor and nonlocomotor skills is essential to the building of a solid gymnastics foundation. Much of modern dance stems from the locomotor skills of walking, running, galloping, leaping, jumping, hopping, and rolling. The sport of gymnastics is also greatly comprised of these same movements. According to Phyllis Cooper (1980), author of *Feminine Gymnastics*, gymnasts will "perform more gracefully and efficiently with a good background in basic movement" (p. 30). Yet, the sad truth is, these steps often receive considerably less attention from coaches than do tumbling and acrobatic skills.

It's true that all gymnasts know how to walk and run and hop by the time they reach the competitive level. If they learned, in addition, a variety of dance walks, these same gymnasts would be able to move with poise and fluidity, for an aesthetic and confident appearance. Similarly, each time a gymnast performs a run as part of a routine, it should be smooth, even, and graceful. The hop, which is included in many of the latest compulsory floor and beam routines, should be correctly executed, with legs turned out, toes strongly pointed, and upper torso erect throughout. These movements may be considered common and unexciting, but when accomplished flawlessly and combined with impressive gymnastic skills, the results are remarkable. This, in turn, will lead to not only more visually pleasing performances and higher scores, but also fewer injuries.

Combinations of locomotor skills can also enhance coordination, flow, and rhythmic ability during warm-ups, and, given the proper music, can make lively additions to optional floor routines. For instance, the end products of many combinations are steps derived from folk dance, opening up whole new avenues of possibilities. A two-step is simply step, close, step. A schottische consists of step, close, step, hop. The basic polka requires a hop, step, close, step.

The following are descriptions of selected locomotor movements used often in gymnastics. As previously mentioned, there exists today a great cross-fertilization between dance styles. All of the movements described in this chapter, therefore, are likely to be seen in the performances of any of the three techniques. However, there are some steps and movements more readily associated with one form of dance than the others. The following are generally associated with modern dance.

Walk

Instructors spend a good deal of time on the walk in many beginning modern dance classes. It's not that students don't know how to walk but that a dance walk should not resemble the average walk witnessed on the streets (unless that's what the choreographer desires). The same point can be made with regard to gymnastics.

A basic dance walk is executed with the legs slightly turned out and the toes of the feet pointed. Good posture must be maintained, with the head held erect and the eyes focused straight ahead. Shoulders are relaxed and down, but the arms may be held in any number of positions. The principal difference between a dance walk and a normal walk, however, is the placement of the feet upon the floor. In the latter, the heel strikes the floor first. In a dance walk, the toes and then the ball of the foot are placed upon the floor, with the heel following (toe-ball-heel). Although the rhythm or tempo of the walk will be determined by the instructor or by the choreography, the movement must normally be smooth and easy. The gymnast who masters this fundamental locomotor movement will have a definite advantage in the performance of all movements.

Run

Much of the above description can be applied to the run as well. The average run is executed heel-ball-toe, but, in dance, the reverse must once again be implemented. Generally, the dancer and the gymnast will be expected to perform a run in turn-out. With many dance runs, the performer is in a slight *plié*; so the run is lower to the floor than usual.

Gymnasts must sometimes use average running steps as preparation for a tumbling pass. When a run is called for in compulsory or optional floor exercise, however, it is a dance run that the judges expect to see. In optionals, the gymnast has a wide range of choices in the type of run performed, from one executed in *plié*, with the back leg being dragged just a bit on the floor, to one executed in *relevé*. Arm positions can also vary greatly, from holding hands on hips to swinging arms in opposition to the legs, with the head turning in opposition to the arms. A series of runs might connect a tumbling pass to a finishing pose or a series of *chaîné* turns to a Hecht jump. In general, two points must be kept in mind about the run. First, a series of runs should be used *only once* in an optional routine, as any more than that may be seen as taking the easy way out. Second, regardless of the type of run performed—average or dance, in whatever style—the gymnast must take *all* body parts into consideration, including the eyes, which should be focused at whatever level the choreography designates.

Jump

A jump propels the body upward from a takeoff on two feet. The toes, which are the last to leave the ground (heel-ball-toe), are the first to reach it upon landing, with landings occurring toe-ball-heel and in *demi-plié*. Jumps are used frequently in gymnastics, in a wide variety of ways. For descriptions of the tuck, Hecht, and stretch jumps, among others, refer to chapter 3.

Hop

A hop is a movement that propels the body upward from a takeoff on one foot. The landing is then made in *demi-plié* on the same foot, toe-ball-heel. The free leg does not come in contact with the ground.

The definition sounds simple enough, but it is not enough for the gymnast to know the mechanics alone. Legs that are supposed

Figure 5.1   Hop

to be straight must be *completely* straight. Toes must point when in the air. Takeoffs and landings should be smooth and cleanly executed. The upper torso should remain lifted throughout, hips squared and level, shoulders down, arms controlled, and eyes focused at eye level. That's quite a bit to concentrate on for such a small movement, but one of the goals of modern dance is mastering the small movements so that the big ones eventually pose no problem.

A number of variations are possible with the hop. Three variations that are used in compulsories are (a) a hop with the free leg in parallel *retiré* (see Figure 5.1), (b) an *arabesque* hop with the free leg extended at a 90-degree angle to the back, and (c) a hop with the free leg extended at a 90-degree angle to the front. Other possibilities include holding the free leg in turned out *retiré, sur le cou-de-pied,* or in *attitude.* The hop is also quite versatile in that it can be performed in place or while traveling in any direction.

Roll

When gymnasts hear the word *roll,* they naturally tend to think in terms of forward or backward rolls, both of which are used often in floor and beam routines. But a roll is generally defined as a movement made by a body that is supine or prone and fully extended, with arms stretched overhead. Of course, that type of roll would be difficult to execute on the balance beam; but if a gymnast were looking for a locomotor movement that would contribute to the use of a low level in space, a dance roll could be the perfect choice on floor.

Lots of variations of the dance roll are possible with a little imagination. The gymnast could initiate the roll by the upper torso alone, giving the movement a twisted effect. In another variation, the gymnast could first perform a typical roll, followed by one in which the knees contracted toward the chest so that the gymnast completed the movement in a kneeling position. Alternatively, the gymnast could use a change in arm positions, for example, a bending of the arms so the backs of the hands are directly in front of the shoulders and elbows are held tightly to the side of the body. Then, at the completion of the roll, with the body prone, the gymnast could push off the floor with the hands, arching the back and lifting the face toward the ceiling.

Leap

Leaps, known as *jetés* in ballet, are described in chapter 2. Side, stag, and switch-leg leaps, used more often in jazz dance, are described in chapter 3.

Gallop

A gallop is a locomotor skill that, unlike those above, is performed with an uneven rhythm. It is executed in much the same manner as a *chassé* in which one foot always leads and the other plays catch-up. With a gallop, however, the gymnast is not required to spring into the air, toes pointed, as the back foot meets the forward one; and because the gallop is used in modern dance rather than in ballet, there's room for experimentation. A gymnast might perform a gallop with small body waves, giving the torso an undulating effect, or use gallop turns, executing one full turn after every forward step. The gymnast can also perform a small series of gallops in a zigzag path, alternating the forward foot. He or she could even make use of a backward gallop.

Skip

A skip is actually a combination of two locomotor skills—a step and a hop. Like the gallop, a skip consists of an uneven rhythm. With more emphasis placed on the step than the hop, the overall effect is that of a light and skimming motion during which the feet only momentarily lose contact with the ground. The gymnast might choose to use such a movement when portraying a carefree feeling, gaily swinging the arms in opposition to the free leg. Or the gymnast could incorporate large skips into a routine, pushing further off the floor and lifting the free leg to *retiré* on each hop. Skips can also be performed backward or while turning and can travel in straight, curving, or circular paths. They are most appropriate with a musical accompaniment in a 6/8 meter (refer to ''Varying Rhythms'' in chapter 6).

Step-Hop

Although a step and a hop are the components of a skip, the skip's rhythm is uneven because the accent is placed upon the step. In a step-hop, the accent is equal on both the step and the hop, so the rhythm is even. For instance, a step-hop might be more appropriate when the floor exercise music is in a 2/4 meter, as each bar consists of two quarter notes of equal value. A step-hop has a heavier feeling than a skip and might therefore be used in a routine with an earthy or folkdance flavor.

Waltz Step

If gymnasts are accustomed to working only with even rhythms, it's important to include a waltz step as part of dance training. Performed to the accompaniment of a 3/4 meter (**one**-two-three, with the accent on the one), the waltz step is most easily practiced while moving in a straight line across the floor. Taking a step forward, the gymnast *pliés* on the count of ''one'' and then lifts to *relevé* for the final two steps. The motion, therefore, as the feet step right-left-right, will be down-up-up (see Figure 5.2). The gymnast should also practice beginning the movement on the left foot. Once the

Figure 5.2 Waltz step

basic step is mastered, variations should include stepping up-up-down (*relevé-relevé-plié*), and incorporating a full turn into the original movement.

Nonlocomotor Skills

Some locomotor skills, such as the hop and the jump, are occasionally performed in place, traveling upward only. Even the walk and the run can be performed in one spot, though this is seldom the case in gymnastics. Both modern dance and gymnastics also make frequent use of such nonlocomotor movements as bending, stretching, twisting, turning, and falling—performed both as movements unto themselves or in conjunction with various locomotor skills.

Stretch

Murray (1975) defines a stretch as "a full extension of any part of the body in any possible direction, on a vertical or horizontal plane or any point between"(p. 131). This definition is perhaps more fully realized in gymnastics than in any other activity. In compulsory routines, gymnasts are required to stretch arms, legs, torsos, and even necks. They must perform stretch jumps and stretched poses, and execute fan kicks, *grand battements*, and split leaps, each of which stretch various parts of the body. Despite its common occurrence in gymnastics, there are several creative possibilities for this nonlocomotor movement, including the following: a high stretch followed immediately by a collapsing swing of the upper torso and arms can add an element of surprise to a routine, both arms stretched to the same side can add interest to a pose, and a lower torso bent in *plié* with a fully stretched upper torso can add contrast. Gymnasts should note that inhaling deeply with a stretch and expelling the breath at its conclusion can add even greater contrast to such movements.

Bend

A bend brings two adjacent body parts together, generally toward the body's center, and is made possible by ball-and-socket or hinge joints. Bent legs, arms, and waists play a major role in both dance and gymnastics, but even if no other uses were made of the bend, dancers and gymnasts alike would be thoroughly familiar with it because of their experience with *pliés*.

Bending and stretching are natural partners because, once a body part has bent, it must eventually straighten again. In dance, the two work together to create specific effects. In a *développé*, for instance, the leg rises to a bent position before stretching to a full extension. Similar contrast is evident in a tuck jump, where the upper torso is stretched but the lower torso is bent.

Experimentation with bent body parts can eventually result in some interesting poses and movements. The gymnast might occasionally (*intentionally*) make use of a flexed foot. An arm bent at both the elbow and the wrist can give a movement or pose an Egyptian look. A pirouette in *plié*, with the free leg bent at both knee and ankle, would be unusual but might be quite appropriate for a certain passage of music (one perhaps consisting of very low notes). A turn incorporating a sideward bend at the waist could create a startling, off-balance impression.

Rock and Sway

Although both the rock and the sway share the common trait of transferring weight from one part of the body to another, they are essentially different. A rock is the more forceful movement of the two, using greater muscle tension and suspension. A sway is an easy, relaxed motion in which suspension plays a minor role.

If including a rock in a routine, the gymnast should be certain that the movement is controlled and balance is maintained, particularly if used on beam. As mentioned, a rock is a forceful movement and can be effectively employed in contrast to lighter movements. A sway, for example, could suddenly be transformed into a rock. A rocking motion could also be used as a lead-in to a fall, in which the gymnast purposely loses balance in order to change levels in space. A sway could be used in optionals as an alternative to yet another body wave.

Turn

A turn is a rotation of the body around an axis, and there may be no end to the number of ways in which that movement can occur.

In gymnastics alone, there are inside turns, outside turns, turns on two feet, turns on one foot, and turns on no feet at all (turns in the air). Included in these categories are *chaînés*, pirouettes, *attitude* turns, *fouettés*, *tour jetés*, turning jumps, and the like.

For any turn to be successful, there are some common denominators that must be applied. First and foremost is proper body alignment: The hips must remain over the supporting foot (or feet), and the shoulders must be in line with the hips (if the body is bent or arched during the turn, the shoulders will not be over the hips but must still be in line with them). The torso must be both tight and lifted, from the buttocks up; arms must be controlled; and the gymnast must use spotting. Without all of these elements, the audience and judges are likely to see a gymnast who merely whips the body around (because the routine calls for a turn at that point), hopes for the best, and normally falls out of the turn before its completion.

In addition to those turns with which the gymnast is already familiar, there are countless others that can be employed in optional routines. A turn that incorporates a contraction might be used just prior to a stretch jump, providing contrast between the contracted body and the lifted one. A turn that begins on the floor and spirals upward until the gymnast is standing is an effective way to change levels in space. A *tour en l'air* that lands on one knee provides both contrast and a change in levels.

Twist

Modern dancers believe in showing their audiences lots of bodily shapes. There is perhaps no more enjoyable way to discover the range of bodily shapes than through the use of twisting. Because arms, legs, and even the upper torso and head can all twist, there's no end to the ways in which gymnasts can use this nonlocomotor movement. For a corner pose just prior to a tumbling pass, for instance, a gymnast might twist at the waist, hands on hips and head twisted in the opposite direction from the upper torso. A gymnast could momentarily twist at the waist while in midair with a split leap. The hips can twist briefly in imitation of the famous dance from the 1950s and 1960s; or the arms can twist, adding an extra element to a shimmy of the shoulders. Gymnasts composing optional routines should be careful not to become too abstract with their movements and poses, but that shouldn't keep them from experimenting.

Side Fall

Once perfected, a fall can be a safe and effective way to change levels during a routine. But, as expected, there is a very specific way to execute it. The gymnast must begin with the weight supported primarily on one foot, with the other foot crossed behind it and raised to half-pointe. The fall will occur in the direction of the free leg. The gymnast's torso, therefore, is leaning slightly that way; but the weight of the head, which is tilted in the other direction, acts as a brake.

The side fall is initiated by the arms, which lift away from the body (in the direction of the fall), over the head. The upper body and arms lean toward the opposite direction of the fall; the arms swing across to the front of the body, and the knees bend to lower the center of gravity. The gymnast then rolls onto the side of the thigh while sliding the arms out to the side. As the arms approach the front of the body, the head also swings across the chest, in the direction of the fall, and the body begins its drop to the floor. The secret, though, is to perform the movement as a *slide*, by lowering the center of gravity and rolling onto a broad muscle area such as the hip. The hands and the side of the knee reach the floor at approximately the same time, and the hands continue to slide along the floor until the body is finally lying on its side.

Contracting and Releasing Skills

Modern dance makes use of the spine in ways quite different from that of ballet. This is related to the belief that any bodily shape is appropriate, as long as it expresses what the choreographer wants to say. It is further related to Doris Humphrey's principles of fall and recovery, and to followers of the philosophy that energy emanates from the center of the body. But it is particularly the result of Martha Graham's teachings concerning contraction and release. These teachings provide students with a feeling for contracting and releasing various muscle groups. This, in turn, increases strength and flexibility, helps lessen unnecessary tension, and results in greater ease of movement.

Martha Graham's lessons, therefore, are of special significance to gymnasts. Contractions are required in many compulsory floor and beam routines. A proper contraction also adds completeness to body waves, which are used frequently in compulsories and optionals. The following are descriptions of three nonlocomotor activities that require contracting and releasing skills. All are commonly used in both modern dance and gymnastics.

Contraction

Although it may be executed to the side, it is the contraction from front to back that is the most common, particularly in gymnastics. In this movement, the back is sharply rounded, the sternum pulls down and back, and the pelvic area tilts up (see Figure 5.3). It is a common error for the beginner to attempt a contraction using only the upper torso.

Figure 5.3 Contraction

Teaching Hint: Students will better understand the force and feeling of this movement if they can imagine that a fist is about to hit them in the stomach. If such were the case, their reflexes would naturally cause them to contract all of their muscles toward the center of the body, involuntarily backing away from the force of the fist. That is what a contraction should feel like.

In a side contraction the movement takes place primarily at the waist. The waistline pulls inward, on the side on which the contraction is occurring, while the rib cage is pulled down and the hip is pulled up. The feeling is that of gathering all the muscles toward the center, but the movement is to the side of the body rather than to the front.

Modern dancers continue to discover that the use of a sudden, sharp contraction can add an unexpected flair to an otherwise ordinary movement. In a dance with male and female partners, for instance, the female dancer might leap into the arms of the male and suddenly contract just as she's caught. Although such an example cannot be applied to gymnastics, gymnasts composing optional routines might benefit from similar experimentation with unusual uses of the contraction. They could perhaps discover that a side contraction in the course of a pirouette would add just the right element to a routine, or that a quick, double contraction (front to back) could make an effective contribututic to the moment just prior to a tumbling pass.

Cat Back

The cat back is actually a component of both the contraction and the body wave; yet it is also a movement unto itself. The cat back requires moving from an arched to a rounded spine, can be executed in any number of positions, and is an excellent exercise for adding suppleness to the back.

As a movement in optional routines, a cat back can be performed while kneeling, standing, or sitting. It can lead into a full body wave. It could take a gymnast from a kneeling to a sitting position, beginning with the arched spine while on the knees and contracting to a rounded spine that ends with the gymnast sitting on the heels. Cat backs can even be performed while crawling on all fours, combining a nonlocomotor with a locomotor skill.

Chest Lift From Floor

Lying flat on the back, the gymnast arches the spine and lifts the chest toward the ceiling. With the slight assistance of the hands pressing on the floor, the gymnast rises to a sitting position, leading with the chest. The head, which remains dropped to the back throughout, completes the movement by returning upright (see Figure 5.4).

Figure 5.4 Chest lift from floor

This is yet another activity requiring the fluid use of the spine. It is a requirement in some compulsory routines and is often used in optionals to move from a lying to a sitting position. A gymnast could also incorporate the cat back into the movement by performing a chest lift from the floor (arched spine), rounding the back once in a sitting position (rounded spine), and contracting back to the floor. Although some gymnasts find it difficult to lead with the chest, adequate experience with the arched position and with contraction and release should cure that problem.

Improvisational Skills

Although much of modern dance stems from basic movement, it is the variety of ways in which these movements are performed that gives the technique its artistry. This variety comes about through improvisation and experimentation. This aspect of modern dance, therefore, can be closely related to movement exploration (described in the last chapter).

Through improvisation, the gymnast can discover that he or she needn't perform a hop blandly, when it's possible to alter its tempo or to change its look with unusual arm positioning. A gymnast can perform a run smoothly or in a punctuated manner, incorporating stops and starts. Similarly, he or she can strike a pose at a variety of levels, in a variety of shapes. The gymnast can execute any movement, in fact, in any number of ways by exploring the possibilities. In chapter 4 we looked at variations of a walk, in relation to the six elements of movement. The gymnast could further experiment with using the qualities of movement (described later in this chapter) to alter a walking step until the ultimate result was a walk suited perfectly to the gymnast and the choreography. This kind of experimentation would also certainly earn credit for originality.

But variety in routines is only one result of improvisation. It may even be the least significant—because improvisation will also help develop both self-expression and an enhanced ability for performing before an audience. Self-expression is an essential element in gymnastics. Rather than being mere imitations of one another, gymnasts must express individuality and self-confidence to excel. By the same token, the ability to perform before an audience does not mean simply *doing* a routine. It means doing it with ease and letting the audience see and feel that it's a pleasurable experience (not a nerve-racking one!).

Performance and self-expressive skills, in other words, can only result from the confidence that comes from *moving*—moving often, moving well, and moving creatively. If creative, inventive movement is to become a reality, the dance instructor must place as much emphasis upon improvisation with the competing gymnasts as is placed upon movement exploration with the preschoolers.

Naturally, with gymnasts at the competitive level, self-consciousness is likely to be more prevalent. But it can be overcome, and the gymnasts eventually will look forward to the fun; and while they're having fun, they'll be deriving the same benefits that movement exploration offers to young students.

Teaching Suggestions

As with movement exploration, developmental progression plays an important role in improvisation, and instructors should keep in mind and use accordingly the three general progressions cited in the last chapter. For instance, the preschooler must begin by exploring movement as an individual; but older gymnasts are likely to find greater enjoyment and challenge in partner and group work. Improvisation that involves mirroring or shadowing the movements of a partner is both stimulating and fun, and it also serves to avert self-consciousness because participants are not acting singly. Similarly, instructors should include challenges involving laterality or the isolation of body parts. In fact, experimentation involving the head or arms alone can make a major contribution to the creative use of these parts in floor and beam routines. Also, whereas it would make little sense to ask a preschooler to "walk as though anxious," a request such as this might be just challenging enough for a gymnast at the competitive level. The concern is less with beginning at the beginning and more with keeping participants interested and challenged; however, a request such as "walk as though anxious" should still be saved until ample experience with improvisation has alleviated self-consciousness.

There are a number of beneficial activities that can initially be presented to the gymnasts as games, thereby relieving any anxiety caused by the terms *improvisation* or *movement exploration*. The following are examples of partner and group activities that fall into this category. Not only will they contribute to the gymnasts' creativity, but because they're performed with others, gymnasts will be more willing to give them a try than they would solo improvisation. The activities are presented here in progressive order, beginning with the least complex.

Palm Touch.   Performed in pairs, this activity requires gymnasts to consider the number of shapes they can assume with their arms and hands. Facing a partner, who is standing close enough to touch, the first gymnast assumes a shape with his or her arms. (Any shape is acceptable as long as palms face the partner.) The partner then forms the identical shape, bringing hands palm to palm with those of the first gymnast. As soon as contact is made, the first gymnast chooses a new arm position, and the activity proceeds accordingly. Both partners should have the opportunity to act as leader.

Variations: Instructors can make this activity more challenging by asking the gymnasts to form different bodily shapes to go along with the shapes of their arms. The partners must then imitate the body shape (as if they were a reflection in the mirror) prior to touching palms. This will provide experience not only with arms but with the entire concept of shape.

Touch and Move.   This activity requires pairs of students to connect various body parts, designated by the instructor, and to determine in how many ways they can move, despite the limitation. Body parts can include hands (one of each person's, on the same or opposite sides), elbows, knees, tops of heads, and ankles. This is a good problem-solving approach to improvisation that can result in creative solutions to such other problems as changing levels on a four-inch beam or finding an unusual way to move from one point to another on the floor mat.

Variations: Rather than designating body parts, the instructor might simply ask the students to connect a certain number of parts. For instance, the gymnasts might be instructed to connect any two parts or any three parts, or the instructor might ask them to connect different body parts (i.e., one person's foot to the other person's knee). The instructor can also assign spatial restrictions, in which the gymnasts are required to find only an up-and-down way to move or a side-to-side way to move.

Add-a-Step.   The class is divided into two or three groups, each of which forms a line behind the leader. The leader in each group must perform a dance step of his or her choice and then go to the end of the line. The second person repeats the leader's step and then adds one before going to the end of the line. The third person executes both of the previously performed movements, followed by an additional step; and so forth. For gymnasts who have difficulty remembering long movement sequences, this is a first-rate activity for stimulating the memory. Because they must contribute steps that connect well, the gymnasts' flow and choreographic abilities are also enhanced.

Variations: Setting specific limits to the gymnasts' movements can help make this even more challenging. For example, the gymnasts can be asked to perform only movements that can be executed in three counts. Even more difficult would be to limit the overall number of counts for an entire series (for instance, twenty-four counts for one pass through the entire line of students). Another option is to specify what kinds of movements are to be performed. For example, the gymnasts might be required to move alternately in three different ways (e.g., nonlocomotor skill, locomotor skill, and dance step; or dance step, nonlocomotor skill, and gymnastic element).

The Machine.   Problem-solving as it relates to nonlocomotor skills is the principal objective behind this activity. One student begins by continuously performing any movement that can be executed in one spot. A second student then contributes a second movement, which is in close proximity, and relates in some way, to the first movement. For example, if the first gymnast is executing an up-down motion, from *plié* to *relevé*, the second gymnast may choose to do the reverse, standing beside the first gymnast. As these movements continue, each remaining student adds a functioning part to the machine they're building with their actions. The gymnasts may choose any movements at all, as long as they don't interfere with the actions of others and they contribute in some way to the machine.

Variations: One simple variation is to ask each student to perform a sound to accompany the motion. The sound should be something that the gymnast considers appropriate to the movement being performed. This is not only more fun, but also serves to loosen up those gymnasts with a tendency toward self-consciousness. Another more difficult alternative is for the gymnasts to combine locomotor with nonlocomotor skills to create their machine. For example, the first student might begin by walking in a small circle, and the second student might circle outside the first in the opposite direction. The contribution of the third person could be standing in place, a short distance from the other two, repeatedly bending at the waist and straightening. The fourth contribution must then be a movement, locomotor or nonlocomotor, that relates to but does not interfere with the others (such as hopping toward and then away from the center circles).

The Qualities of Movement

Just as there are six elements (described in chapter 4), there are six different qualities, or kinds, of movement, which also play a vital role in improvisation. Sometimes known as *movement dynamics*, the six movement qualities are explored in depth in serious modern dance training. The reason is that the modern dancer must present variety to an audience. In addition, the dancer must be aware of—and capable of performing—the type of movement that best expresses the choreographer's message (e.g., percussive motion would probably be inappropriate for a piece depicting quiet solemnity).

Variety is equally important in gymnastics, and poses a potential problem for gymnasts. This is especially true on balance beam, where there is no music to initiate a change in dynamics. Routines, therefore, sometimes consist of one, or possibly two, qualities throughout.

It is on floor, however, that *expression* plays the largest role. Because there is music involved, a mood or a theme is established from the moment the first notes are played. Therefore, gymnasts need to develop a sense of knowing what type of movement will work with the accompanying music—whether it's movement that parallels the music (sustained motion with a sustained chord), or movement that creates a specific effect by its contrast to the musical accompaniment.

Although an optional routine shouldn't consist of a hodgepodge of dynamics, careful selection can contribute to both variety and expression in an exercise. A gymnast with experience in all six qualities (in addition to the six movement elements) will be one who moves well, no matter what form the movement takes. Dance instructors, therefore, should provide gymnasts with ample opportunity to improvise with the qualities of movement defined below.

Swinging.   Swinging motion takes the form of an arc or a circle around a stationary base. It generally requires impulse and momentum, except perhaps when the swinging part is merely released to the force of gravity. Swinging movement can be executed by the body as a whole, by the upper or lower torso alone, and by the head, arms or legs.

There are a number of swings required in compulsory beam routines, including forward and backward swing turns in which the leg is the principal swinging part, swinging mounts and dismounts, and swings of the body as a whole. Many of the same factors that contribute to a well-executed turn can be applied to well-executed swings. Proper body alignment is necessary for good balance, the torso should be tight and lifted when erect, and free body parts must be kept under control. There should not be so much control, however, that the performer appears reluctant to let go, as a lack of restraint can be a plus when executing a swing.

If mastered, swings can make effective contributions to optional routines as well. A series of side swings of the arms and body that ends in a fall can be an interesting change of levels. Swings of the head (as detailed in jazz isolation exercises) can show the judges that this vital body part has not been forgotten. Finally, swings are wonderfully appropriate for use with a musical accompaniment in a 3/4 meter.

Percussive.   Percussive movement is similar to bound flow in that it is punctuated and accented. A head moves percussively when it drops sharply forward and then back to center. Feet move percussively when they run. Hands and arms move percussively when they perform boxerlike movements. Hips move percussively when they move abruptly side to side, and shoulders when they ''hit'' to the front or back.

As one example, a gymnast might perform three quick punches into the air (percussive movements), open hands and arms abruptly to second position and then gently lower them to fifth (sustained movements), and then perform a tumbling pass (percussive movements). This sequence provides contrast in dynamics (percussive to sustained to percussive), which shows the judges that the movements have been well thought out. Gymnasts who are quite balletically inclined should be especially encouraged to experiment with percussive movement.

Vibratory.   This quality relates to movement that is tremulous or quivering. Images that depict vibratory movement are bacon sizzling in the frying pan, a leaf quivering in the wind, an electric toothbrush, and a baby's rattle being shaken. Body parts that can depict vibratory movement might be a rapidly shaking head, a hand with opened palm and extended fingers trembling in the air, or shoulders moving in a rapid shimmy.

Because vibratory movement is quick, it works well in contrast to slow movement or no movement at all. For example, a shaking hand that suddenly freezes momentarily in midair can be quite effective. Vibratory motion might also be used in conjunction with collapsing movement, as when a body is simultaneously shaking and collapsing toward the floor.

Sustained.   Sustained movement continues through time and space without stopping and, whether slow or fast, requires considerable control. It is usually, however, associated with slow movement—and even slow motion—as when an arm gently and gradually opens from fifth to second position. Movement that is slow and sustained, therefore, works well in contrast to rapid movement, whether it be swinging, percussive, or vibratory. Through improvisation, a gymnast might discover a passage that alternately swings, sustains, and then moves into percussive motion. For example, a forward-backward swing of the body and arms could suddenly come to a stop, with only the arms continuing slowly to the back and overhead. As the arms continued their downward movement, finally reaching the position where they're extended forward, the gymnast could take two quick backward steps, arms simultaneously punching one-two to the front. Sustained movement is most difficult for both the gymnast with a tremendous amount of energy and power, and the self-conscious gymnast who does not feel comfortable with dance.

Suspended.   In suspended movement, the body acts as a base of support, above which one or more parts are temporarily interrupted in their flow of movement. The movement begins with an impulse, reaches its peak of elevation, holds momentarily, and then continues once again. A swing might include a momentary suspension with the arms overhead before resuming the swing again. Suspended movement involving the whole body requires a great deal of control, like sustained motion, in order to maintain the necessary balance. Therefore, proper body alignment is once again a factor to a successful performance.

Any movement can be temporarily suspended in order to achieve a particular effect. Even a walk that is paused momentarily and then resumed can be impressive when used in the right circumstances. Dance teachers, then, should occasionally—and unexpectedly—instruct their students to freeze and then continue.

Collapsing.   Collapsing can be likened to movement that occurs when a puppet is released from its strings, or when a building is demolished. A collapse of the human body, however, must always be executed with the necessary control to avoid injury. In addition to the body as a whole, other body parts can collapse, including the head (collapsing to chest, back, or shoulder), an arm (which has been suspended and then collapses through space), or the upper torso (collapsing toward the lower torso).

Collapsing movement is most often practiced in relation to suspended or sustained movement. A high stretch onto *relevé*, with arms suspended overhead, could suddenly collapse to add both surprise and contrast to a routine. The pattern could even be continued, with the collapse turning into a swing that once again suspends overhead and then proceeds into a sustained, swaying motion from side to side.

Improvisation in Gymnastics Training

Improvisation and movement exploration needn't be the sole domain of the dance teacher. In fact, by using a problem-solving or improvisational approach to the instruction of gymnastics skills, the coach can encourage gymnasts to think creatively, thus contributing significantly to their self-confidence. Even in those cases where a choreographer is secured to compose optional routines, gymnasts with improvisational experience will be better qualified to make suggestions and changes that incorporate their own unique styles, thereby producing more personalized routines.

Essentially, an improvisational approach means only that a coach must ask a lot of questions. While directing practice, coaches can ask gymnasts to combine skills that travel diagonally across the floor mat. For instance, rather than merely requiring students to perform front walkovers from corner to corner, coaches can instruct them each to combine any three skills that move them from one point to the other. An instruction, for example, to combine a locomotor skill, a dance step, and a gymnastic element might result in a skip, a series of *chainé* turns, and a dive roll. During the choreographic process, if a gymnast working out a beam routine executes three running steps, the coach might ask if the run can be performed faster or slower to achieve a certain effect. Might the run be executed in a more punctuated, percussive manner? Can the gymnast find an unusual arm position to assume while running?

Summary

Modern dance is indeed a part of gymnastics, as both locomotor and nonlocomotor skills play a major role in gymnastics. Neither modern dance nor gymnastics could exist, in fact, without such movement. Both gymnasts and modern dancers are also required to be familiar with, and adept at, contracting and releasing skills. Regular practice with these skills is expected of even the most experienced dancers and should likewise be expected of all gymnasts. Finally, it is through improvisation and a constant striving for creativity that modern dancers and gymnasts alike will continue to be able to provide their audiences with performances offering variety, interest, and excitement.

Chapter 6

© Dave Black

The Dance Class

What does a coach or gymnastics director look for in a dance instructor? What sort of instructor is most suitable for teaching dance to gymnasts? What should dance teachers take into consideration when deciding whether or not they would like to become involved in gymnastics? These are the questions reviewed in the first section of this chapter. The remainder of the chapter includes a discussion on class content, offering suggestions for the ideal dance class as well as a sample lesson plan, and recommendations for the use of music during the dance class.

Choosing the Dance Instructor

Earlier in the book, I stated that if only one style of dance could be offered to gymnasts, that style should be ballet. However, the preceding chapters have also outlined the considerable value of jazz and modern dance. Therefore, if a gym is presently without a dance instructor and is looking to find one, the first criterion should be that the instructor have the ability to teach all three techniques, even if the coach is determined to place a strong emphasis on ballet training. This shouldn't pose a problem, given that there is no lack of dancers who've been trained in all three styles. Even if the search for a suitable instructor requires extra time and effort, the coach and the gymnasts will benefit greatly from its results.

A distinction must also be made between the terms *dancer* and *dance teacher*. Unfortunately, they are not always synonymous. A dancer may be a brilliant technician and an absolute wonder at physical self-expression, but it doesn't necessarily follow that she or he can transfer these abilities to others. In a field where dance is not always eagerly anticipated by the students, this fact is of particular importance. Therefore, the gymnastics director should seek out someone with teaching experience and an ability to relate to young people—in addition to dancing talents.

The ideal situation would be for every gym to have gymnastics coaches with extensive dance training or to hire dance instructors with gymnastics experience. This is not always possible, however, and is not of absolute necessity. The prime consideration is that dance teachers be well-versed in their own craft, but they should also possess a willingness to learn how gymnastics and dance interrelate. For example, they'll need to know what dance skills are components in compulsory floor and beam routines. Which dance skills need to be emphasized in order to improve gymnastic technique? What can they offer their students in order to make them more injury-free? In addition, if required, they should be willing to learn to choreograph optional routines.

The gymnastics director must also take into consideration one additional characteristic that is not usually found on the average resumé. If potential dance teachers are to have maximum success in working with gymnasts, they must also possess one final trait: the willingness to be a bit unconventional in their methods (Pica, 1985). Gymnastics requires a unique blending of art and sport.

As mentioned in chapter 1, gymnasts who are already performing advanced dance skills as part of their compulsory routines often find it unnecessary—and rather boring—to spend time on *pliés*, *relevés*, and other such basics. The instructor, therefore, must not only have a certain amount of patience with this attitude, but should also have a knack for overcoming it. The fact is, boredom is simply not conducive to learning. Bored gymnasts will perform the exercises by rote, only because it's demanded of them. But more and more research indicates that the best and most lasting learning experiences are those that are actively sought. So if dance teachers are to make their knowledge more appealing to those gymnasts who aren't interested in acquiring it, they're going to have to make the learning fun!

The essential ingredient required is flexibility. For instance, the teacher may occasionally have to be open to last-minute changes in a lesson plan. Young people always have their favorite activities, and if a gymnast asks to repeat one from a previous lesson, the instructor should remember that repetition is also critical to learning. It gives students the opportunity to once again experience something at which they previously succeeded or to better themselves at something that they felt needed improvement.

If a gymnast makes a suggestion as to the performance of a certain activity, what better indication is there that at least one student is interested and involved? If participants feel they have something to contribute to class—that it's their dance class, too—the instructor is bound to see more positive results.

Finally, dance teachers who choose to work with gymnasts must bear in mind that dance is *their* love, not the gymnasts'. Although dancers can hope to instill a caring and respect for their craft into an occasional student, they mustn't expect it from all of them; for they are gymnasts, and tumbling and vaulting are what they love and what they want to be doing. Therefore, budding dancers may thrive on the order and predictability of the conventional dance class, but these particular students aren't likely to share those feelings.

Selecting Class Content

The traditional ballet class consists of three segments: exercises performed at the barre, exercises performed in the center of the floor, and exercises performed across the floor. In most modern and jazz dance classes, students spend some time at the barre, but they generally perform warm-up exercises at center, both on the floor and standing. These exercises are usually followed by movements performed across the floor (often on a diagonal from corner to corner), with the remainder of the class spent learning a choreographed dance routine (commonly referred to as a *combination*).

If the gymnasts' dance instructor is to be nontraditional, however, the lesson plan must be nontraditional as well. Gymnasts have special requirements, differing from those of other dance students. So, for their purposes, it's best to divide dance classes into a greater number of components. This will not only serve the purpose of covering all critical areas, but will also dictate that each segment be relatively short. Even the most reluctant gymnast can make it through a least favorite section if it's of short duration.

The Warm-up

The lessons should begin at the barre if there's one available at the gym. The barre provides stability, balance, and a sense of proper body alignment essential to students without extensive ballet experience. Exercises performed regularly here should include *pliés*, *relevés*, *tendus*, *dégagés*, *développés*, *rond de jambes*, *port de bras*, and *grand battements* (refer to chapter 2). Sometimes, when there is no barre available, balance beams can be adjusted to the proper height (slightly below shoulder level) and used instead. Gymnasts can also stand alongside a free wall with one hand lightly placed on it. This does not give the inside arm the same placement that it would have on a barre, however, and students may be even more inclined to rely on a wall for support than they would on a barre. Therefore, the dance instructor will have to make a determination as to whether or not using the wall is to the gymnasts' advantage. The above exercises require greater strength and effort when performed in the center of the floor. So, if a particular group of gymnasts does not possess the necessary strength and experience, using a wall or balance beam may be the best choice. Regardless of where they're performed, several or all of these exercises should be part of every warm-up.

The point of a warm-up is to increase the flow of blood to critical areas of the body, to promote flexibility, and to ensure against injury. However, it is also intended to contribute to strength, rhythmic ability, and the development of technique. In a dance class for gymnasts, the warm-up should do all of this and provide students with the greatest possible movement vocabulary. Exercises, therefore, should always be performed to a rhythmic count (with and without music), be selected from all three dance techniques, and cover the body from head to toe! The following is a list of significant body areas and parts, along with suggestions for specific exercises. Students should perform these exercises in addition to the balletic exercises mentioned earlier:

Neck. Head isolations (refer to chapter 3).

Arms. Arm circles; also jazz combinations emphasizing coordination and rhythm.

Shoulders. Shoulder isolations (refer to chapter 3).

Waist and Upper Torso. Stretches with arms alternately reaching toward the ceiling; stretches from side to side, with arms in second position; side stretches with arms reaching across the body; side stretches (arm over the head) while sitting in a straddle position.

Hips and Outer Thighs. Hip isolations (refer to chapter 3).

Ankles and Feet. Pointing and flexing feet while sitting or standing; ankle circles; exercises that isolate toe, ball, and heel.

Inner Thighs. Stretching in a straddle position, including nose-to-knee and chest-to-floor stretches.

Hamstring Muscles. "Pretzel" stretch (illustrated in Figure 6.1).

Figure 6.1 "Pretzel" stretch for hamstring muscles

Calves. Calf stretches (see Figure 6.2).

During the warm-up segment of the class, the instructor can also concentrate on turns, contractions, body waves, jumps in place, swings, lunges, and combinations involving two or more movements. If slight variations occur from week to week, with a progressive skill development in mind, gymnasts will appreciate the variety and will feel both challenged and accomplished.

Obviously, a warm-up that incorporates all the necessary ingredients requires a rather fast-paced block of time. Unfortunately,

Figure 6.2 Calf stretches

time is of the essence for gymnasts and their dance instructors, with many gyms scheduling only an hour a week for dance. Therefore, if the gymnasts will be going right into practice after class, or if the dance class includes strenuous gymnastic elements, they should be completely stretched and ready to perform strenuous skills. Such a warm-up, however, is not the responsibility of the dance teacher, whose time with the gymnasts is already so limited. The solution, then, is for the gymnasts to arrive at the gym in time to stretch out sufficiently *before* dance class begins.

Moving Across the Floor

Gymnastics, like dance, involves a great deal of locomotion. Therefore, a crucial segment of the gymnasts' dance class is the execution of movements across the floor. This time is devoted to such steps as *chaîné* turns (including proper spotting), *fouettés, tour jetés*, and leaps (e.g., split leaps, stag leaps, *sissones*, side leaps, switch-leg leaps, and *pas de chat*). Also included in lesson plans should be triplets, waltz steps, dance walks and runs, grapevine patterns, *chassés*, and slides. Finally, such basic locomotor skills as skipping and hopping should not be overlooked.

In addition, this is the time to present the gymnasts with the challenge of movement sequences. Drury and Schmid (1973), authors of *Introduction to Women's Gymnastics*, believe that the practice of two or three moves together is more beneficial than executing a single movement. They state that the performance of short sequences accustoms gymnasts ''to the feeling of continuity required for a fluid routine'' (p. 17). Coordination and rhythm are enhanced, and the result is an exercise that is ''light, graceful, and alive, and consequently beautiful'' (p. 17).

Fostering Creativity

The next period of the class should be devoted to creativity. For gymnasts, this is often the most popular segment, particularly for those who feel uncomfortable with the restrictions placed upon them by someone else's (their dance teacher's) style. It may even be the most important part of the class, offering benefits beyond those results witnessed during floor and beam routines.

In this period, the instructor and the students are limited only by their imaginations (and, to some degree, by the age of the participants) with regard to the ways in which creativity can be developed. I have already cited several appropriate ideas in the chapters on movement exploration and modern dance. In addition, the more experienced students might be given an assignment to create their own individual, partner, or group dances, based on a movement element or quality, a particular theme, or a piece of music. (Instructors should remember that, in the beginning, they can alleviate self-consciousness by dividing the class into groups of no fewer than three students.) Depending on the assignment, the dance may be completed and displayed during one class; or it might be continued for several weeks. In the latter case, the gymnasts should be given weekly opportunities to show their pieces. This will not only demonstrate their progress, but also teach them a great deal about performing for an audience.

Dancing

In the next segment of the class, the students should learn a dance (or combination) that the instructor has choreographed. Although it's extremely important for gymnasts to tap their own creative potential, it's equally beneficial for them to be exposed to a movement vocabulary outside their own and to be able to imitate physically what they're seeing.

Choreographed dances also give the teacher an opportunity to provide additional instruction in specific dance skills in a manner generally more appealing to the gymnasts. In other words, if they've been reluctant to learn steps as part of a warm-up, simply for the sake of learning them, the instructor should bear in mind that these students are particularly movement-oriented. So, because they'll find actual dancing more fun than learning, they'll be more inclined to master steps—those same steps they found unappealing during warm-ups—used within the context of a dance. Learning takes place more readily when students enjoy the lessons. Thus the dance class should consist of as much dancing as possible; but there's no reason the dancing can't be composed of steps and skills the gymnasts need to learn!

Cooling Down

Because muscles contract during exercise, it is equally important to stretch them following movement. Some of the same exercises used during warm-ups, therefore, can be practiced during cool-downs. Such exercises might include *demi-pliés*, and stretches for the waist, thighs, and hamstring muscles. Calves especially should be stretched.

Breathing exercises can also play a significant role in a cool-down. One of the principal reasons for a cool-down is relaxation, and breathing exercises certainly promote relaxation. A simple example is to ask the students to raise their arms overhead as they inhale slowly and deeply through the nose. Then the students lower their arms as they exhale slowly through the mouth. Alternatively, students can stand in parallel first, in *demi-plié*, bent at the waist with their heads lowered as close to the floor as possible. As they roll-up, one vertebrae at a time (keeping chin to chest and back rounded), they inhale through the nose, straightening their legs as they rise. The reverse is then executed—rolling down chin to chest, bending the knees, and exhaling through the mouth. This exercise not only promotes relaxation but stretches the back and hamstring muscles as well.

A Sample Class

As mentioned, many gymnasts are exposed to a mere hour a week of dance. Though it may not seem so to the gymnasts, an hour can be an incredibly brief amount of time for the dance teacher trying to do the best possible job. Even if the cool-down were just two minutes, there would be only 58 minutes remaining for the other four segments described above, or 14 minutes and 30 seconds per segment, which is just barely adequate. Therefore, based on the information contained in this book, as well as the needs of the gymnasts in question, coaches and dance teachers must work together to determine priorities. Priorities can change, however, and should be periodically reviewed as the gymnasts progress.

The following is a sample lesson plan that gives attention to all of the segments outlined above (the particular emphasis in this lesson is on turns). It is assumed that the gymnasts in this class have had experience with the various components and will require little correction in the execution of the steps. With a well-prepared lesson plan, the teacher can keep the class moving (literally!) at a smooth, quick pace. Not only will this ensure that the planned material is covered, but the gymnasts will also appreciate the ease with which they progress from beginning to end.

I. Warm-up
  A. At barre: *demi-pliés, tendus, dégagés, port de bras* (refer to chapter 2).
  B. At center: head and shoulder isolations (see chapter 3), standing stretches for waist, toe-ball-heel isolations (jazz), calf stretches (lunges), inside and outside pirouettes from a lunge position.

II. Across the floor
  A. Turns: *chainé* and galloping.
  B. Combination: combine *chainé* and galloping turns with any nonlocomotor skill performed between them.

III. Creative
  A. Divide gymnasts into groups not divisible by three; form lines.
  B. Play "Add-a-Step," adding a different turn with every third step.

IV. Dance
  A. Add 16 more counts to last week's combination.
  B. Review and rehearse complete combination to date.

V. Cool-down
  A. Gentle swings: side-to-side and front-to-back, incorporating *plié* and *relevé*.
  B. Roll-downs with breathing, calf stretches, and roll-ups with breathing.

Music in the Dance Class

Although it's important for students periodically to explore and experience movement on its own, activities using music are bound to be more fun than those accompanied only by the teacher's verbal instructions. Most exercise leaders will vouch for the fact that there's no greater source of motivation than a musical beat. So, if fun and motivation are to be part of the gymnasts' dance classes, instructors must give careful consideration to the use of music.

Providing Variety

Variety of music is critical, both from the gymnast's and from the teacher's point of view. Variety will not only help maintain interest, but also familiarize students with musical elements they might not otherwise encounter. As a result, they will learn to feel comfortable with moving to various kinds of music. The following are examples of different musical elements to help the dance instructor select pieces offering ample variety.

Styles.   Style is a difficult word to define. In music, one style generally differs from another in the way the elements of form, melody, harmony, sound, and rhythm are treated. For the most part, however, people can judge one style from another. Rock and roll, for example, certainly differs from opera—though the majority of listeners would have trouble verbalizing the reasons why. There are many rhythmic styles from which to choose, and all are likely to inspire different types of movement.

For example, Scott Joplin's *The Entertainer* (ragtime) would produce choreography substantially different from Samuel Barber's *Adagio for Strings* (a classical piece of the 20th century), though both have been used as movie themes. Dance teachers, therefore, should provide opportunities for gymnasts to play the game of "statues" to various styles of music (see chapter 4, "Exploration With Music"). If choreographing a piece to one style of music one month, they should choose another style in the next. Other musical styles that merit consideration are jazz, folk, country and western, blues, rhythm and blues, disco, gospel, swing, and Dixieland.

Periods.   Naturally, it would take an extensive course in music history to cover all that past ages have produced. Classical music alone consists of a number of periods. By offering gymnasts a selection from each, the instructor can provide them with a tremendous amount of variety.

From the Rennaisance era, for instance, came pieces such as *Greensleeves*, played at Christmastime under the title, *What Child is This?*. Bach's many works were products of the Baroque era, as was Pachelbel's lovely *Canon in D-Major*. From the Classical period came Haydn's *Surprise Symphony* and Mozart's *Eine Kleine Nacht Musik (A Little Night Music)*. Next came the Romantic period, with Prokofiev's *Peter and the Wolf*, the Strauss waltzes, and Tchaikovsky's *Swan Lake, Nutcracker Suite*, and the forceful and expressive *1812 Overture*.

All of the aforementioned pieces easily lend themselves to movement, as do those belonging to the decades of American music. The twenties, for example, were the years for the Black Bottom, the Charleston, and other such flappers' delights. The thirties ushered in an era of Latin rhythms. The forties produced the big bands and their particular brand of swing. Elvis Presley was a product of the fifties, which saw the beginnings of rock and roll. During the sixties, young people were performing such "solo" dances as the swim, the pony, and the mashed potato to the accompaniment of Top 40 hits. And the seventies, with disco, saw the return of partner dancing.

Nationalities.   The world is peopled with hundreds of nationalities, and each has its very own musical heritage. There are Polish and Mexican polkas, German and Austrian waltzes, Italian tarantellas, Irish jigs, Scottish Highland flings, and English folk songs. There's African chant and drum music, calypso, reggae, and the Jewish hora. There are Latin rhythms, Greek dances, East and American Indian songs, and many, many others. All of these inspire different kinds of movement.

Textures.   Although it may come as a surprise to some teenage gymnasts, songs don't always consist of vocals, backed by guitar, bass, and drum. Nor does every instrumental number have to be orchestral. Exposure to varying textures will mean that gymnasts become accustomed to hearing and moving to sounds produced by different instruments. Dance teachers should make every effort to use as many different textures as possible, in as many segments of the class as possible.

For example, a piece consisting only of percussion instruments (an African piece, perhaps) is likely to produce movement that is percussive and staccato. In contrast, a violin sonata by Brahms would generally tend to result in balletic or legato motion. Other musical textures would be created by solo piano, brass, woodwinds, voice alone (a cappella), electronic instruments, acoustic guitar, and harp.

Meters.   Students must also be aware of meters other than 4/4, the most commonly used meter in music (and certainly in Top 40 music). Other meters that should be used in class are 2/4 (found in polkas and many marches), 3/4 (used most often for waltzes), and 6/8 (found also in marches and in many folk songs).

Experience has shown that students whose classes are conducted strictly to pieces with a 4/4 beat (with movements counted in fours and eights) often have a difficult time hearing, feeling, and moving to the swing of a 3/4 meter. Gymnasts must have this ability if they are expected to vary the qualities of their movements on floor and beam. There are also some very interesting qualities that can result from exposure to less common meters, such as 5/8, 7/8, 12/8, and 5/4. Though undoubtedly more difficult to find, these meters will inspire movement that will be well worth the effort.

Other Elements.   There are other musical elements that gymnasts should encounter in dance class. The first are those involving tempo: slow, fast, accelerando (music that begins slowly and gradually becomes faster), and ritardando (music that gradually decreases in tempo). The second group relates to the movement element of force: soft and loud, and crescendo and decrescendo (volumes that gradually get louder and softer, respectively). Lastly, the element of flow is explored through music that is either staccato (accented, punctuated) or legato (smooth and flowing).

Providing Motivation

Warm-ups, then, might be performed to the beat of Top 40, rock, and jazz rhythms easily counted in fours and eights; swinging exercises (and waltz steps across the floor) to 3/4 meters; and isolations to perhaps Latin or African rhythms. One week the gymnasts might be required to learn (or create) a dance accompanied by *Little Nash Rambler*, an example of accelerando that was a popular song in the 1950s. The next week the instructor might choose Bach's *Little Fugue* and the following week, *The Skater's Waltz*.

Finally, the flexible instructor is bound to produce more favorable results by occasionally using music contributed or suggested by class members. Naturally, the students' tastes in music may not coincide with the teacher's, but dancing to music that they've chosen can only enhance the gymnasts' enjoyment. Again, the more pleasant a learning experience, the more the students will gain from it.

Summary

Exposure to all of the material outlined in this chapter will not only help gymnasts to broaden their movement vocabulary and perfect their technique, but also will play a vital role in their ability to express themselves. Team members are frequently told to sell a routine, to show it off, or to present themselves to the audience. But with so much time devoted to skills acquisition, little concentration is given to teaching gymnasts *how* to show it off—how to *perform*. The responsibility, then, rests with both the dance teacher, who must choose the class content, and the gymnasts, who must form the habit of physically expressing themselves every time they move. This means that during dance classes, even the exercises must be *felt* and *performed*, rather than simply conducted by rote.

Chapter 7

Choreographing Floor Routines

© Dave Black

The gymnast's first step in choreographing a floor routine is to consider which movements, sequences, and/or tumbling passes to include. But by far, the most important step for female gymnasts is the selection of music: the routine really can't begin to come together without the musical accompaniment. Because it's critical that the movements and music enhance one another, careful thought must go into choosing a floor exercise piece.

Because male gymnasts do not perform floor routines with musical accompaniment, their rhythmic needs are actually more similar to the female gymnasts' choreography needs of beam routines (see chapter 8). The special dance training needs of male gymnasts are addressed in chapter 9.

The first topic of this chapter, therefore, is the selection of music, both commercially prepared and personalized. The remainder of the chapter deals with the choreography itself. Although this book does not attempt to provide step-by-step instruction, it does offer several elements of composition for consideration by gymnasts, dance instructors, and coaches. These elements are intended to provide gymnasts with floor routines that not only meet requirements but also display to audiences and judges the best the gymnasts have to offer.

Choosing Music

Generally speaking, it's best for the beginner to select a commercially prepared (prerecorded) musical accompaniment from a gymnastics dealer or company specializing in music for floor exercise. Such companies offer a choice of records and cassettes, consisting of several pieces suitable for varying ability levels and movement styles. When listening to these, however, gymnasts and their coaches should give serious consideration to a number of factors.

The first factor will be the appeal of the piece. Unless it's something the gymnast truly likes, she won't be able to give the impression that she's enjoying herself (Pica & Gardzina, 1984). Regardless of whether her piece is whimsical or dramatic, if a gymnast doesn't enjoy her performance, she cannot sell it to an audience. Also, considering how often she's going to hear the music during the course of a season (and normally two or three seasons!), she had best be *very* enthusiastic about it at the start, because even the most popular songs tend to lose their appeal when played often enough.

Without exception, the gymnast's personality must also be taken into consideration. No matter how much she might like a particular selection, a gymnast with a serious and dramatic nature would look unnatural attempting a performance with a cute and lively theme. A gymnast with a reputation for being class clown might well choose music on the lighter side.

The same applies for the girl's physical stature. Is she small and lightweight, or strong and powerful? What amount of stamina does she possess at that point in her career; what is her technical ability? If she'll be unable to withstand long passages of nonstop movement, both her music and choreography must be carefully chosen to allow her the necessary rests. By the same token, it would probably be best if her routine were closer to the minimum time allowed (one minute and 10 seconds) than to the maximum (one minute and 30 seconds).

Another important factor concerns whether or not the piece contains contrasts in rhythm and style. Music that never changes is not only unexciting for an audience to listen to, but also doesn't offer the gymnast a chance to display her ability to move in a variety of ways.

Finally, does the piece consist of a clear and distinctive melody and rhythm? If it doesn't, it will be difficult to use in a noisy or acoustically poor gymnasium. It will also come across as little more than background music, similar to that heard in restaurants and elevators. A gymnast must avoid music that will do nothing to enhance her movements, or to contribute in any way to her performance.

Preparing a Personalized Tape

There may well come a time in a gymnast's career when she decides to display her talents on floor with the help of a specially prepared musical accompaniment. Here she selects a song (or songs) from which segments are extracted and pieced together, in the order of her choice, to form a suitable floor exercise tape. The gymnast's music must comply with FIG requirements, but it will still be a piece she can call her own.

For the gymnast who wishes to make such a statement, the factors outlined in the above section must still apply. In addition, there are a number of other elements she'll have to consider. These elements, listed below, do not appear in any specific order, as they are all of equal importance.

1. It is stated in the *Code of Points* that floor exercise music must include changes in quality. When a gymnast purchases a commercially prepared piece, such changes are normally built into it. But when the choice of music is the gymnast's, she must remember this particular requirement and avoid repetition of rhythm and tempo (and even melody or use of the same instrumentation) throughout.

"Changes in quality," however, is not meant to imply that the piece should be a mixed bag. On the contrary, there should be an underlying theme. Or, if varying themes are used, they should have some musical element in common. If so, transitions are more likely to fit together musically and to be smooth and undetectable.

2. Whenever possible, segments should be chosen from just one song (if that song has the necessary contrasts within it). This ensures a similar feel and likeness in the overall sound of the recording, as well as continuity of theme throughout the piece. When more than one song is used, it's best that they be performed by the same artist or artists, and preferably from the same album.

3. The introduction should be carefully selected. Often a gymnast will pick an introduction she likes that has no relation to the rest of the piece. Because the introduction establishes the theme of the routine and helps create that important first impression, it's advantageous for it to be linked in some way to what follows.

4. The music should lead into and out of each tumbling pass, and should be timed to correspond to the length of the pass itself. Tumbling can be so much more exciting when the music accompanying it is more clearly dynamic than the rest of the piece. This can happen when the gymnast has an approximate idea of how many seconds it takes to complete each of her passes *before* her music is prepared.

5. The required change in musical quality should not be accomplished by inserting into the middle of the piece several seconds of slow music that has no relation to the rest. Often a theme is established, only to be suddenly interrupted by a passage of music that has been stuck in for the sole purpose of providing a change in tempo. That, too, is then ended as quickly as it began; and the original theme (or a similar one) is resumed. The impact of this is jarring when flow and continuity should be the goal.

6. When possible, the ending should leave the judges and audience with a feeling comparable to that experienced upon reading the words *The End* at the completion of a book or movie. In other words, both the music and movement should finish *satisfactorily*. In general, music that fades out will be less effective than that which ends on the perfect note or chord. However, if a fade-out can't be avoided, it can be enhanced by the accompanying movement (such as one that also sustains and then fades). If the music is to have a definite conclusion—and it's not the actual ending of the song being used—the gymnast should be especially careful that her finishing notes don't sound chopped off. In gymnastics, last impressions are as important as first impressions.

7. If the gymnast takes the time to select carefully the components of her piece, then she should go the full route and be sure those components fit together with the smoothest possible transitions. This usually means seeking the help of a professional musician, who'll transfer the music from records to reel-to-reel tape. From there, the pieces are spliced together (hopefully with a puzzlelike fit), and finally transferred to cassette. Transitions are

sometimes made smoother with the help of additional instrumentation performed by the musician.

Regardless of whether floor exercise music is commercially or personally prepared, quality is always of the utmost importance. Name-brand cassettes are worth a bit of extra expense because cheaper tape deteriorates at a much faster rate. Also, a piece recorded directly from the speakers of a record player to the microphone of a tape recorder is going to be cluttered with unwanted noise, whereas using the line inputs and outputs of a cassette deck and amplifier will ensure clarity of sound. This will not only enable the gymnast to hear her music clearly (even in noisy gyms), but help instill in her the desire to achieve quality. If she sees that time and effort have been spent in providing her with music of a professional nature, she'll almost certainly have a stronger desire to do it justice.

Elements of Composition

Once the gymnast has her floor exercise music, where does she go from there? In many ways, this is dependent upon the gymnast who needs the choreography. Some (normally those who've achieved a certain skill level in both gymnastics and dance) are perfectly capable of composing their own routines from beginning to end. But, most often, either the coach is responsible for all choreography, or the job is delegated to the dance instructor. In some cases, a choreographer is hired just for the purpose of creating floor exercises.

Complementing Music and Gymnast

Regardless of where the responsibility lies, there are two very important elements to be considered before any composition is begun. The first is that the choreography must complement the music. As obvious as that might sound, it's not impossible for choreography and music to clash. For instance, if the gymnast selects music based only on the fact that she likes it, it could very well require movement that she is incapable of performing, because of either its style or its level of energy.

The second point, then, naturally follows—that the choreography, like the music, suit the gymnast. To begin, the gymnast's personality, level of ability, and stamina must be contemplated. What is her predominant style of movement? (For the most part, this should have determined her choice of music.) What are her strengths and weaknesses? How can the former be emphasized and the latter avoided? (This question must be asked with regard to tumbling, acrobatic, and dance skills.) Is she strong enough to perform her most powerful tumbling pass near the end of the routine? How can she use her talents to make the best possible first and last impressions?

It is not enough, however, for the choreographer to merely be familiar with the gymnast. Although familiarity certainly helps, the gymnast herself should still be allowed as much input as possible into the routine's composition. She should try out movement passages as they're designed and be allowed to create passages of her own—or to make suggestions for changes in steps — whenever possible. After all, the most brilliant choreography in the world will only be as effective as the gymnast's ability to perform and express it.

Creating the Routine

If the gymnast is using personalized floor exercise music, then her tumbling passes should already have been designed. Planning dynamic musical passages to coincide with tumbling can be especially effective. If this has not been done, however, the first step in composing the floor routine is to plan the three tumbling passes based on the gymnast's strengths and abilities, and using the three most dynamic parts of the music.

Then it is simply a matter of filling in between the passes, using the answers to the questions above and the remaining music. At this point, some choreographers and gymnasts prefer to create movement segments comprised of those skills at which the gymnasts excel, in addition to required moves and difficulty elements. They must then adapt these sequences to suit the musical accompaniment. Others prefer to let the music itself provide the inspiration, improvising and experimenting until satisfied with the results.

However it is achieved, the next step is to fit the pieces together, joining dance and acrobatic series to tumbling passes so that the composition flows smoothly from beginning to end. Naturally, the skills must complement one another, and the transitions must be executed effortlessly. This is a potential weakness in a routine; if a gymnast does not give attention to transition, her routine may call for first dancing and then tumbling and then dancing again. Every movement should be carefully considered and chosen. If a pose or a less strenuous movement is used in order to provide a bit of rest, it must enhance the preceding and following movements. The same applies to those steps that may have to be added so the choreography coincides with the length of the accompanying music.

Spatial Requirements

Although a great deal of the work has now been accomplished, the floor routine is still far from finished. There is, to begin with, the element of space to consider. How, in other words, will the gymnast use the allotted floor space to perform her exercise? Gymnastic requirements specify that she cover as much floor area as possible, incorporating a balanced and creative variety of pathways, directional changes, distances covered, and levels. She must lay out her routine accordingly, bearing in mind the following:

- Tumbling passes, although generally performed on the diagonal, should not all originate from the same corner.
- Dance and acrobatic sequences should be planned to move across the center of the floor, along the edge of the mat, or along curved or zigzagging paths, to offset the use of the diagonals.
- Direction changes should not occur in corners only.
- The gymnast must not remain in one spot for very long, or return often to one area of the floor.
- Series of movements should be planned so they do not all cover the same distance.
- Movements performed close to the floor (in a lying, sitting, or kneeling position) must be incorporated to offset the high tumbling and leaps, and to fulfill the requirement for level changes.

Many times it's helpful to draw a floor plan on paper (see Figure 7.1), because it enables the gymnast or choreographer to actually see whether or not the above requirements have been met. If the requirements haven't been met, the necessary changes can be more easily made in pencil and then transferred to actual performance.

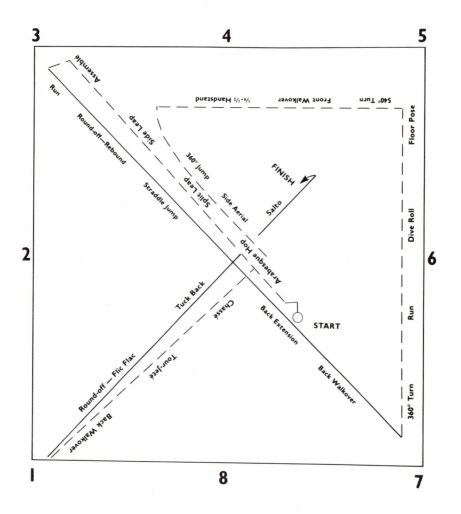

Figure 7.1 Diagram of Class II compulsory floor exercise, 1985-89, reprinted by permission of American Alliance for Health, Physical Education, Recreation & Dance, 1900 Association Drive, Reston VA 22091

Compositional Checklist

Finally, once the above spatial requirements have been met, it's critical that the gymnast (and choreographer) review the entire exercise with the following checklist in mind. The gymnast alone is ultimately responsible for providing honest answers to these questions, because it's her score, after all, that will depend on them.

1. Have required dance, tumbling, and acrobatic skills and difficulties been incorporated into the piece?
2. Are the difficulty elements spaced throughout the routine? If the most difficult elements appear at the beginning, the judges will expect even more difficult skills to follow; consequently, they will have to make deductions for faulty distribution.
3. Is the gymnast performing up to her capacity? Working up to capacity is expected, but attempting to exceed it will only lead to poor performance. The authors of *Judging and Coaching Women's Gymnastics* (Bowers, Fie, & Schmid, 1981) state: "A rule of thumb is to insure that the movement is performed well in at least eight out of ten tries over a span of at least ten workouts before even considering its use in the competitive situation" (p. 164).
4. Are there rhythm and tempo changes?
5. Are transitions between elements smooth?
6. Has the gymnast made use of her whole body?
7. Does the routine display a variety in movement qualities (refer to chapter 5)?
8. Does the routine build to a climactic finish, without attempting something the gymnast may be unable to attain at the end?
9. Are all pauses in the exercise carefully planned? Do they contribute to the choreography, as well as providing a bit of rest?
10. Do the opening and closing movements and poses make a statement in relation to the rest of the piece? Do they provide effective first and last impressions?
11. Are the music and movement in harmony with one another?
12. Is the gymnast performing in harmony with both of the above? Is her personality evident? Her style? Is she demonstrating both ease and enjoyment?

Summary

The gymnast should be allowed as much choreographic input as possible if the piece is to succeed. Therefore, she should have the option of accepting, rejecting, or modifying the suggestions of the coach or choreographer. If all of the spatial requirements have been met and the gymnast can answer yes to the questions above, her floor routine is bound to stand out in the crowd. It will accomplish everything the judges could demand of it, and it will be a routine unlike any other because it will be a statement of her unique personality.

Chapter 8

Choreographing Beam Routines

© Dave Black

According to Margit Treiber (1973), "Of the four international gymnastic events, the balance beam routine is the most difficult to choreograph interestingly and perform successfully" (p. 45).

Treiber wrote those words nearly 15 years ago. Today, despite the increased element of risk found in many beam routines, the choreography for this event is still often relatively unexciting. This is due, in large part, to a lack of originality in three general areas: movement selection, use of space, and use of varying rhythms.

Movement Selection

Because nervousness plays such an overwhelming role in the performance of beam routines, the gymnast must consider her strengths and weaknesses when preparing her balance beam choreography. To start, she may find it helpful to make a list of the skills she's capable of performing in the areas of mounts, dismounts, dance (e.g., leaps, turns, locomotor movements, etc.), static positions, tumbling, and acrobatics. She must then ask herself which of those listed she can realistically expect to master on the high beam prior to her first competition.

Having made such a list, the gymnast's first step in the choreography is simply a matter of beginning at the beginning—with the mount. Which of the mounts on her list would she most like to use? Taking into consideration the importance of first impressions, she probably wants to choose the mount with the highest point value, *if* it's one she'll be able to perform consistently. A strong, steady mount is going to get her off to the best possible start.

The gymnast must then decide how she'll move out of the position in which the mount leaves her. The movement must not be awkward or overly complex and should lead logically and smoothly toward her next skill. A jump from the side of the beam to a squat position, for instance, leads more naturally into a one-quarter squat turn and then a forward roll than it would into a stretch jump. Proceeding in the same manner, the gymnast carefully chooses every movement so that it flows into the next. Of course, she must also consider FIG rules and requirements, and she should bear in mind the following points:

- An exciting skill such as a back handspring or side aerial will be far more effective if the gymnast chooses the movements immediately preceding and following the skill to embellish it.
- The gymnast should alternate inverted and upright movements for variety.
- Occasionally focusing to the side or on a diagonal, beyond the beam, will break up the monotony of constant focus on the beam's ends. One manner in which this can be achieved is by beginning or ending one or more turns on a diagonal.
- Only three stops are allowed during the course of a routine, including skills such as handstands, splits, or scales. Hiding stops by standing still while moving only hands and arms is now strictly forbidden. The trunk or feet must be in motion, or it will be counted as a stop. Poses, therefore, must be carefully selected.
- The gymnast can use a variety of movement elements and qualities in contrast to one another to create interest and excitement. For example, a quick forward movement might be immediately followed by a slow sideward step. Or, a motion

begun in a slow, sustained manner might finish suddenly and forcefully. (Refer to chapters 4 and 5.)

- Movement should involve all body parts: head, shoulders, arms, torso, legs, and hips. Too often, the gymnast holds the head erect throughout an entire routine and uses arms and legs only in the most common ways (arms are frequently used for balance only). Experimentation with the elements and qualities of movement will ensure the creative use of various body parts.
- The routine should display a variety in the locomotor skills used. Not all connecting or traveling movements should be running or walking steps. The gymnast can select from hops, turns, slides, leaps, and jumps. By the same token, not all leaps and jumps should be preceded by a preparatory run or *chassé*.
- The gymnast should demonstrate flexibility and balance through the use of selected movements and poses.
- The gymnast should space difficulties throughout the routine.
- The gymnast should choose only those movements that can be executed with maximum control and balance. A solid, stable performance is the ultimate goal of any beam routine.

The last point applies to the dismount as well. When selecting her dismount, the gymnast should certainly strive for an element of difficulty. But if she is to leave the judges with the best possible last impression, her dismount must be difficult *and* solid.

Use of Space

Perhaps the greatest challenge in composing and performing an original, exciting beam routine is in creatively using the limited space available. The apparatus is, after all, only 16 feet long by about 4 inches wide. Therefore, the possibility of monotony is considerable. The following points, then, warrant a good deal of consideration during the choreographic process.

- Of foremost importance is the fact that every pass should not move across the entire length of the beam. Passes should sometimes cover only one-third, one-half, or three-quarters of the apparatus.

- Turns and jumps should not only be spaced throughout the routine, but also occur on varying parts of the beam. Too often they are used only at the ends for the purpose of changing directions.
- If a pass is meant to cover the full beam, it should do exactly that and not leave unused inches at the extreme end.
- All skills such as walkovers and cartwheels should not be performed in the same direction. Nor should they always be executed in the middle of the beam. Performing such movements at the very end of the apparatus contributes an element of risk and excitement to an exercise.
- Occasionally, movements performed at the beam's extreme end should face *outward*. Such movements might include scales, kicks, turns, body waves, and contractions.
- Sideward and backward movement should be incorporated into the routine, as well as positions that cross or are oblique to the apparatus.
- The creative use of tucked and piked body positions can contribute greatly to a routine's spatial content.
- Changes in level are a requirement in beam routines. To use the lower levels, the gymnast can plan movements that require lying on front or back, kneeling, squatting, lunging, or sitting. Certain movements may even be performed below the beam. Although leaps, jumps, and tumbling skills make use of a higher level, stretches and occasional movements performed in a strong *relevé* can provide additional variety. Sudden changes in level will also add to the routine's success.

Varying Rhythms

In a balance beam routine, rhythm is often considered second only to technique in importance, perhaps because beam routines do not incorporate music to assist those gymnasts without a natural sense of rhythm. In addition, performing rhythmically in such a restricted area, elevated approximately four feet off the floor, is extremely difficult. Perhaps, then, this difficulty factor is the reason that points are deducted for both monotony in presentation and lack of rhythmic variety (e.g., uniform tempo during the entire exercise or during a long passage). Gymnasts, however, can use certain techniques during both the choreographic process and practice sessions to ensure changes in rhythm.

If the gymnast gives appropriate consideration to the different elements and qualities of movement as she is composing the exercise, rhythmic changes will be guaranteed. For instance, earlier examples under "Movement Selection" spoke of a quick forward movement followed by a slow sideward step. In this case, the element of time is used to produce both contrast and a change in tempo. Similarly, a motion begun in a sustained manner and finished forcefully will result in a shift in tempo. A gentle swinging motion will differ in rhythm from a series of sharp, percussive movements. A movement that suspends and then collapses also results in a change of rhythm. The gymnast, therefore, should be familiar and comfortable with all of the elements and qualities of movement. Although she will not want her routine to consist of an overwhelming assortment of qualities, careful selection will naturally result in a rhythmically interesting performance.

Another technique that can be incorporated during choreography is the use of counts to modify rhythm. One series of movement, for instance, may take four counts, with the following steps using only two, and the next taking five. An example would be a body wave performed to four counts, followed by a tuck jump in two, a cartwheel, and a contraction.

Once the gymnast completes the routine, she may find it helpful to rehearse it to music, varying the accompaniment from one practice session to the next. The pieces used should differ from one another in style and tempo *and* should each consist of some rhythmic variety. A disco number in a constant 4/4 beat, for instance, will do nothing to help create a rhythmically interesting routine. (Refer to chapter 6 for suggestions on how to ensure musical variety.)

Compositional Checklist

Upon completion of the early versions of the choreography, the coach and gymnast will want to review the routine. Although this process is time-consuming, they should give careful thought to the following checklist during the review and provide honest answers, especially on the part of the gymnast. A second such review should take place once the gymnast has a finished product. However, the routine should not be truly considered finished until all of the requirements below are satisfactorily met.

1. Does the choreography include all required steps and difficulty elements?
2. Do the movements and poses chosen offer both variety and excitement (see "Movement Selection")?
3. Have all of the spatial elements been fully considered and used to the greatest advantage?
4. Does the routine offer rhythmic variety?
5. Do the movements flow together without running into one another? Although judges place considerable emphasis on continuous motion, the gymnast must be sure to articulate each movement with a clear beginning and end.
6. Does the routine consist only of skills with which the gymnast has had a suitable success rate? The gymnast should have a 90 percent success rate with skills performed on the low beam before trying them on a beam of regulation height. Likewise, she should have a 90 percent positive performance on the high beam prior to attempting to execute skills during a competition.
7. Does the routine fall within the regulation time of 1:10 to 1:30 minutes? Again, because nervousness tends to play a major role during actual performance, a routine that uses either the extreme minimum or maximum amount of time may default during competition. Those gymnasts who are less experienced should especially avoid such extremes.
8. Has the gymnast's stamina been taken into consideration in determining the length of an exercise? A long routine is best left to those gymnasts possessing the necessary staying power.
9. Does the routine build to a climax? A climactic finish is just as important on the balance beam as it is on floor.
10. Is the exercise presented in such a way as to make judges and audience forget the restricted surface upon which it's performed?
11. Are there any surprises (e.g., unexpected changes of direction, level, or rhythm)?

Summary

If used to its full extent, the information covered in this chapter should result in a beam routine choreographed most 'interestingly'' (Treiber, 1973). Successful performance is yet another matter. It requires creative movement selection, clever use of the limited space, and a brilliant display of rhythmic variety. But even those gymnasts with the most perfectly choreographed routines do not always perform them perfectly, and, generally, the reason for this is not an inability to execute the above elements but a case of nervousness. It's crucial, therefore, that beam routines, like floor routines, be suited to the gymnast's style and personality in every way. If so, the gymnast will have much greater opportunity for success; and the more often she experiences success, the greater the chance that confidence—and not nervousness—will rule the performance.

Chapter 9

Dance and the Male Gymnast

© Dave Black

I discussed in chapter 1 the several arguments to be made for the inclusion of dance training in the gymnastics program. Although the discussion thus far has primarily addressed the female gymnast, many of these arguments apply to the male gymnast as well.

The argument for injury prevention, for example, applies in both instances. Certainly, male athletes can benefit from a knowledge of proper body alignment and the resulting balance and control. In addition, they can profit from the ability to sense and make proper use of the whole foot, allowing for greater stability when on the floor and a greater capacity for springing from it.

Similarly, it's important that male gymnasts acquire mastery over such body parts as hands, arms, faces, and heads. It's critical, for instance, that they learn what to do with hands and arms when there is no equipment to occupy them. As with their female counterparts, males can use faces and heads to contribute to both expression and rhythmic variety. The dance technique of spotting is also invaluable for anyone who must perform turns.

Besides these similarities, there are needs specific to male gymnasts and to their dance training. This chapter addresses these unique needs, including overall body development, and outlines some suggestions for dance instructors whose students include male gymnasts.

Unique Needs

Male gymnasts often possess a weakness that is peculiar to their gender alone. According to Toby Towson (1986b), an NCAA floor exercise champion in both 1968 and 1969, many male gymnasts "have magnificently trained upper bodies, while their legs just seem to hang and go along for the ride" (p. 41). Dance training, he believes, can help the male gymnast to develop his body in a more "harmonious" manner.

However, as it is with the female gymnast, individual expression and creativity can be most greatly enhanced by the addition of dance to the male athlete's training. Men especially find self-expression to be a problem, generally because society has only recently begun allowing males the freedom of emotional expression. In men's competition, floor exercise is known also as free exercise, because gymnasts are free to use the space provided to *express* themselves "through tumbling and transitional elements showing flexibility, strength, balance, and rhythm" (Towson, 1986b, p. 41). Yet most routines are surprisingly similar due to a lack of personal expression, creativity, and music to heighten differences. Therefore, because dance adds to the male gymnast's enjoyment of movement and instills him with poise and self-assurance, it will free him from inhibition and allow him to be more creative.

Of course, once the coach and dance instructor are convinced of the benefits, there is still the problem of a lack of enthusiasm on the part of the gymnasts themselves. As with the females, gymnastics is the chosen extracurricular activity, and male gymnasts also experience a natural resistance to forced participation in something that, in their minds, leaves less time for what they'd rather be doing. In addition, with males there is the problem of image. A sad but true fact is that the male dancer has long been considered unmasculine and even homosexual. Young men who willingly take part in dance classes often have to fight to prove their masculinity to their peers and sometimes to their parents as well.

Fortunately, this has begun to change with the increasing visibility of dance in general and of the male dancer in particular. Popular television shows and movies now use greater numbers of dancers, both male and female, and even offer story lines concerning the lives of those who choose to make their living in this field.

The males depicted are usually in possession of admirable physiques and seem to be anything but unmasculine.

The emergence of breakdancing a couple of years ago was yet another boost for the image of the male dancer. Because breakdancing tended to be performed primarily by young men and was rather athletic in its nature, its popularity helped "to dispel the myth that dancing is only a feminine occupation" (Towson, 1986a, p. 55). Breakdancing also borrowed from gymnastics in its use of flips, pommel horse moves, and front and back handsprings. This fact perhaps makes it especially advantageous to those teaching dance to male gymnasts.

Instructors, however, must keep enjoyment in mind at all times. As discussed in previous chapters, enjoyment is a critical factor to learning, and it may be even more critical where young male gymnasts are concerned—particularly during early efforts.

Teaching Suggestions

The dance style being taught, therefore, is of special significance. If it's a style that appeals to these students, they're likely to put forth a greater effort. The dance style most likely to appeal to them is modern jazz, accompanied by contemporary music. They're familiar with both (probably more than well acquainted with the latter), and that familiarity will lend itself to feelings of comfort and enjoyment.

All warm-up stretches and exercises, then, should be accompanied by music and should have a modern flavor. Isolations, for example (described in chapter 3), should certainly be included in lessons, performed to a stimulating, rhythmic accompaniment. If the instructor wants to include such ballet exercises as *pliés* and *relevés*, they should also be performed rhythmically and perhaps experienced first in parallel positions only, as males especially will feel uncomfortable with turn-out. Similarly, arms should be held throughout these exercises in positions more likely to be comfortable to young men than, say, fifth low. Holding hands on hips or folding arms across the chest may be good starting points, and the men can eventually graduate to a jazz second.

Instructors have to be alert to those areas in which the male gymnasts display weaknesses. Flexibility and rhythmic ability, for example, are two areas in which males may not be as strong as their female counterparts. Therefore, teachers will have to design their lesson plans and choreograph their dances accordingly. Flexibility can be attained through the various stretches outlined in chapter 6, but it must be achieved *gradually*. Rhythm will be enhanced through the use of music in the class, but males especially must be exposed to as many varying rhythms as possible. Although a variety of rhythms is more difficult to obtain through contemporary music only, it is not an impossibility. An occasional use of Latin or African rhythms, in addition to contemporary music, might just spark the students' interest and solve this problem.

Because men's floor routines are not performed to music, they are similar to beam routines in that rhythmic diversity is more difficult to achieve. The qualities of movement, therefore, must once again receive special attention (refer to chapter 5). Men are generally familiar with movement that is percussive, but they must also learn to perform movement that swings, vibrates, sustains, suspends, and collapses. These qualities are perhaps best experienced as part of the dances choreographed by the teacher to end the classes. They might also be incorporated into combinations performed across the floor.

Self-expression, as mentioned, is an area that tends to make men feel uncomfortable, at least until they've had adequate experience with it. However, movement exploration and improvisation aren't likely to provide the solution for male gymnasts—at least not for a good long while. But the instructor can have them use problem-solving when moving across the floor, asking them to create their own combinations of locomotor, nonlocomotor, dance, and gymnastic skills. Even such little exposure to problem-solving will result in enhanced creativity, leading to feelings of success and self-assurance.

The male's dance class, then, need only consist of four segments: warm-up, movement across the floor, dance, and cool-down. Until the men feel somewhat at ease with dancing, the pieces the teacher choreographs should be fairly brief. In fact, to begin with, one half-hour class a week for the men may be sufficient and wise.

Summary

Finally, success is a critical element. As with any student—young or old, male or female—experiencing success is a great source of motivation and inspiration. Achieving it with male gymnasts may mean that the dance instructor has to adopt a slower pace and display greater patience. Alternatively, it may simply be necessary for the teacher to expend greater effort in relating the art of dance to the students' sport. Arnow (1981) summarizes this point well: by frequently relating dance to gymnastics, "through movements common to both, [the teacher] will give the male a type of action he is comfortable with and imagery with which he can identify" (p. 39).

And, in the opinion of Toby Towson (1986a),

When men take the time in their training to learn the basics of dancing, we will see the benefits not only in floor exercise but in...other events, as well. [Dance has] much to offer the gymnast, both in the technique of quality movement and the attainment of self expression. (p. 55)

Appendix A

Sources for Floor Exercise Music

Personalized

Richard Gardzina, 109 Berry River Road, Rochester, NH 03867, 603/332-6917.

Barry Nease, 204 Shrineview Ave., Boalsburg, PA 16827, 814/466-7731.

Sportsounds, P.O. Box 6343, Wyomissing, PA 19610.

Prerecorded

Children's Book & Music Center, 2500 Santa Monica Blvd., Santa Monica, CA 90404, 800/443-1856.

Elite Expressions, 2201 Shad Ct., Naples, FL 33961, 813/775-2921.

Kimbo Educational Records, P.O. Box 477, Long Beach, NJ 07740, 800/631-2187.

Millco Productions, Box 3890, Peabody, MA 01961, 617/535-6125.

Rhythmics, Inc., P.O. Box 492, Commack, NY 11725, 800/237-8400, ext. 492.

Sportsounds, P.O. Box 6343, Wyomissing, PA 19610.

United Productions, P.O. Box 8807, Anaheim, CA 92802, 800/535-1800.

Appendix
B

Music and Materials for Movement Education

Children's Book & Music Center, 2500 Santa Monica Blvd., Santa Monica, CA 90404, 800/443-1856.

Kimbo Educational Records, P.O. Box 477, Long Beach, NJ 07440, 800/631-2187.

Moving & Learning, 109 Berry River Road, Rochester, NH 03867, 603/332-6917.

References

Arnheim, D. (1980). *Dance injuries, their prevention and care*. St. Louis: C.V. Mosby Company.

Arnow, M. (1981). Teaching dance through sports. *Journal of Physical Education, Recreation and Dance, 52*, 39-41.

Bowers, C., Fie, J., Kjeldsen, K., & Schmid, A. (1972). *Judging and coaching women's gymnastics*. Palo Alto: National Press Books.

Bowers, C., Fie., J., & Schmid, A. (1981). *Judging and coaching women's gymnastics*. Palo Alto: Mayfield.

Cayou, D.K. (1971). *Modern jazz dance*. Palo Alto: Mayfield.

Cooper, P. (1980). *Feminine gymnastics*. Minneapolis: Burgess.

Drury, B.J., & Schmid, A.B. (1973). *Introduction to women's gymnastics*. Palo Alto: National Press Books.

Fowler, J.S. (1981). *Movement education*. Philadelphia: Saunders College.

Gelabert, R. (1964). *Raoul Gelabert's anatomy for the dancer (as told to William Como)*. New York: Danad.

Grant, G. (1982). *Technical manual and dictionary of classical ballet*. New York: Dover.

Halsey, E., & Porter, L. (1970). Movement exploration. In Sweeney, R.T. (Ed.), *Selected readings in movement education* (pp. 71-77). Reading, MA: Addison-Wesley.

Jacob, E. (1981). *Dancing: A guide for the dancer you can be*. Reading, MA: Addison-Wesley.

Murray, R.L. (1975). *Dance in elementary education.* New York: Harper & Row.

Penrod, J., & Plastino, J.G. (1980). *The dancer prepares.* Palo Alto: Mayfield.

Pica, R. (1984a). Injury prevention through dance training. *International Gymnast Magazine,* **26**, 58, 83.

Pica, R. (1984b). Oh, those hands and arms! *International Gymnast Magazine,* **26**, 38-39.

Pica, R. (1985). Wanted: Unconventional dance teachers. *International Gymnast Magazine,* **27**, 44-45, 58.

Pica, R., & Gardzina, R. (1984). Choosing your music, Part II. *International Gymnast Magazine,* **26**, 46.

Stearns, M., & Stearns, J. (1968). *Jazz dance, the story of American vernacular dance.* New York: Schirmer Books.

Towson, T. (1986a). Breakdancing and gymnastics. *International Gymnast Magazine,* **28**, 55.

Towson, T. (1986b). Dance training: Imperative for male gymnasts. *International Gymnast Magazine,* **28**, 41.

Trieber, M. (1973). Avoiding monotonous beam routines. In Wallace, L. (Ed.), *NAGWS gymnastics guide, May 1973-May 1975* (pp. 45-48). Reston, VA: American Alliance for Health, Physical Education, Recreation and Dance.

Index

About the Author

Rae Pica is a professional dancer and dance instructor of children and adults. She is a nationally known movement education specialist and author and is creator and director of *Moving & Learning*, a company that produces original materials for movement education. Ms. Pica has written numerous articles on dance and movement for *International Gymnast Magazine*, including "Dance for the Gymnast," "Encouraging Creativity in the Gymnast," "Injury Prevention Through Dance Training," and "Wanted: Unconventional Dance Teachers." Her many articles on movement education for children have appeared in such publications as *Instructor Magazine*, *Preschool Perspectives*, and *Child Care Center*. An accomplished lyricist and vocalist, Ms. Pica has also written *Poetry in Motion: Poems & Activities for Moving & Learning with Young Children*. She writes a column for *Early Childhood Music*, and hosts "Move for a Minute," broadcast on public television stations nationwide.

Rae Pica lives in Barrington, New Hampshire with her husband, Richard Gardzina, who composes and performs all of the music for *Moving & Learning*. In her leisure time Rae enjoys reading, doing needlework, and relaxing by the water at her lakeside home.